History
Meaning and Method

Third Edition

DONALD V. GAWRONSKI
Florissant Valley Community College

CONSULTING EDITOR
Russel B. Nye
Michigan State University

Scott, Foresman and Company

Glenview, Illinois   Dallas, Tex.   Oakland, N.J.
Palo Alto, Cal.   Tucker, Ga.   Brighton, England

Library of Congress Catalog Card Number: 74-79323
ISBN: 0-673-07968-6

Copyright © 1975, 1969, 1967
Scott, Foresman and Company.
Philippines Copyright 1975, 1969
Scott, Foresman and Company.
All Rights Reserved.
Printed in the United States of America.

Foreword

Historians, it is said, are not completely confident that they
can define precisely what history is. This is not a reflection on historians; rather, it means simply that history is as complex, variable,
and puzzling as the people whose lives and acts it records. Like literature, philosophy, and the arts, history is a way of looking at human experience—at the lives of the individuals who are its parts
and at the life of the society which is the sum. What is history's
importance to the United States in the later twentieth century?
What does it have to say of value to a world taut with tensions and
shadowed by doubt?

First, it must be understood that history is a response to the
eternal desire of human beings to know about themselves. For this
reason it is fundamentally a humane study, emphasizing the importance of people, their individual choices, the values they hold, and
the angles of vision by which they have looked at themselves and
the world. This pervading interest in humanity is the vital link between history and other humanistic disciplines with which it shares
tools and objectives. But because history deals primarily with the
human race in *time*, it offers a way of looking at human experience
that the other humanistic disciplines do not: History brings depth
to the study of humanity, giving it a past perspective and a sense
of the inevitability of change. Because history deals with the flow
of things, it shows that nothing stands still, that experience is dynamic and continuous; it lets us know that while what is happening now is important, people have had problems before and have
survived them. One of history's most valuable contributions to its
reader and writer is that it puts the present in its proper place.

Second, history is concerned with societies as well as with individuals. Like social scientists, historians are interested in how—and

hopefully, why—men and women have acted together as social beings. Because of its link with the social sciences, history uses the same hypotheses and findings to observe how people have developed their institutions, what they have used them for, and how they acted within the political, social, and cultural frameworks by which they order their lives. The purpose of the historian, as Marcel Proust once defined that of the novelist, is "to rediscover, to grasp again and lay before us, that reality from which we have been so far removed by time . . . ," that is, to recapture the reasons which lie beneath action by recovering the experience.

Since history is interested in *causes,* it enlarges and clarifies our comprehension of the social process; it tries to provide a more disciplined view of some of the social problems that beset us. There is more than a little truth to Santayana's famous observation that "those who do not know history are doomed to repeat it," for to know how society has operated in the past may serve to remind us of the possibilities and alternatives inherent in the present. History cannot tell the present exactly what to do, but it may help it to avoid making the same mistakes over again. Today's society can distill something out of the past that may be useful for its guidance, for history has a kind of built-in early warning system for those who know how to listen to it.

Third, history emphasizes the uniqueness of human experience, both individual and collective. As we read history, we begin to recognize that life is idiosyncratic and variable and that each piece of it has its own integrity. However attractive the parallels between past and present may be, we soon learn that the past is not really repetitive, that history never does quite repeat itself. History warns us that we cannot trust reiteration, that we cannot say that what worked once, or failed once, will do so again. It serves as a corrective to too much self-confidence and too-easy answers, reminding us that we are very, very human. George Kennan, who turned to the study of history (and won a Pulitzer Prize in it) after a distinguished diplomatic career, once pointed out that in an era of spectacular scientific and technological change, when the planets themselves seem accessible to man, "he needs to be reminded of the nature of the species he belongs to, of the limitations that rest upon him, of the essential elements, both tragic and hopeful, of his own condition. It is these reminders that history, and history alone, can give."

Fourth, while all the humanities have the duty of conserving, transmitting, and interpreting experience, history has the special obligation to recall, reassess, and reinterpret the past, bringing it to bear on the present and translating it into a form each new generation can use. Historians deal, of course, in facts with an actual past, tied to a particular plane of reality and fixed immovably by the iron law of the documented date. But they deal not only in fact but in *feel;* they try to infuse facts with insights into the quality, tempo, temper, and meaning of the life in which they are rooted. Facts, despite the saying, do not speak for themselves; they say something only when chosen, arranged, and interpreted. Albert Bushnell Hart remarked a half-century ago, "Facts as facts are no more history than recruits arrayed in battalions are an army."

More than literature, philosophy, or the arts, history selects and judges. It sifts the whole of human culture again and again, finding new relevance in some segment of experience an earlier generation discarded, putting away for posterity something which for the moment has lost its usefulness but to which some future generation will give new meaning. What the historian must do, to use Samuel Eliot Morison's words, is "to relate the past *creatively* to the present." The purpose of the historian, then, is not merely to locate and understand the facts of human experience, but to transcend them by giving them values that are stimulating, suggestive, and newly pertinent to the historian's own time. That is why history is not only written but rewritten. It is what Emerson meant when in 1851 he wrote enigmatically in his journal, "History is vanishing allegory."

Russel B. Nye

Preface

Several years of attempting to discover a means both of generating student interest in the study of history, even if no advanced courses are contemplated, and of increasing the probabilities of student success in the survey history course have prompted this work. The intent has been to aim at the lower division student, not at the graduate student. Hence, there is absolutely no claim here to supersede or replace any of the several excellent guides to historical method, works on historiography, or studies on philosophy of history.

The material contained herein has been developed solely to serve as a general introduction to American or European survey history courses and to the discipline as a whole. It has not been designed to produce expert historians, but it can provide a solid foundation upon which the art of the historian eventually may be developed. For this, the third edition of the book, all of the chapters have been thoroughly updated, questions for discussion have been appended to appropriate chapters, a new chapter on the historiography of women and blacks has been added, and an index has been provided.

The book is divided into seven chapters. The first deals with a definition of history as a discipline—and there are many such definitions. Chapter 2 is concerned with identifying some of the various problems that are encountered in the study of history. Chapter 3 serves as an introduction to philosophy of history and traces the development of dominant philosophies throughout history. Concerning the methodology of history, Chapter 4 contains materials on types and techniques of historical writing, suggestions for planning and organizing a term paper, and information on the types and use of footnotes. Chapter 5 is concerned with presenting a brief treatment of the development of American historiography, while Chapter 6 attempts to serve the same purpose for medieval and modern European history. Chapter 7 covers the historiography of women and blacks—a new and rapidly expanding area of historical inquiry.

Finally, Appendix A consists of a short bibliographical essay, a bibliography containing a sampling of various types of works that the student may consult for further reading, and a rather lengthy citation of the various guides and bibliographies in the English language to which he or she might refer in writing a basic history research paper or in choosing a book intelligently. To aid in developing time perspective and in obtaining a broad picture of human developments, a time scale for the history of the earth and chronological tables of American and European history are included in Appendix B.

D.V.G.

A Note to the Student

To succeed in a survey history course, you need an understanding of its purpose. The purpose of the survey history course is threefold: (1) to serve as a general introduction to the study of human history; (2) to provide what has come to be known as "general education"; and (3) to establish a solid base upon which to develop historical scholarship, if you discover that you are interested in this field. Basic fact, technique, method, and what Carl Gustavson refers to as "historical mindedness" are both the goals and the justification of the lower division survey history course in the modern college curriculum.

As a beginning student of college-level history, you may encounter two problems that are brought on by the nature of history courses. One of these problems is how you are going to become sufficiently interested in a survey history course so as to want to master the subject matter, some of which you may have already studied several times earlier in your education. The other problem is how you are going to obtain the necessary tools to achieve academic success in any general history course at a level corresponding to your particular abilities.

Both of these problems stem from the fact that, to many college students at the lower division level, survey history courses often appear to be nothing more than memorization courses in names, dates, and events. In the minds of many students (and perhaps you are one of them) history has no intrinsic value or meaning; it possesses only the highly dubious extrinsic value of being a required portion of a degree program—an ordeal which must be undergone in order to advance toward the coveted diploma.

Several reasons may be given for this negative student attitude. For one, you must remember that your instructor is faced with the perplexing problem of presenting a tremendous bulk of material within the rather cramped time period of the average survey course. Instructors cannot cover everything that they would like to cover, nor can they afford to give every student the thorough, detailed preparation for the discipline that they would like to give. There simply is not enough class time available. Consequently, many students feel that history courses consist of a bombardment of facts; this feeling raises a question in their minds—a question the answer to which will oftentimes determine their success or failure—"Why should we study more history?"

Beginning students of college-level history require a thorough orientation to the nature of history as a discipline if they are going to profit from its study; but to provide that orientation, the instructor must sacrifice the presentation of some valuable historical material. Ideally the lower-division student of history should be well equipped to write book reports and reviews; reviews of articles in learned journals; and, most probably, term papers. But this is the ideal; it is often not present in reality. To some students college assignments may initially appear bewildering. The material contained in this book is designed to aid both in saving valuable class time and in answering the fundamental question: "Why should we study more history?"

Expanding class sizes in lecture-type courses rapidly open the way to objectively scored examinations. Essay examinations tend to be reserved primarily for upper-division and graduate history students. On the objectively scored examination, emphasis is often placed on the recall of factual materials—or so it would appear. This lends credence to the notion that history is a sheer memorization course, for memorizing often seems to be the primary requirement for passing the course. As a student, you must be made aware of the significance of history if you are going to become sufficiently receptive to profit from the lessons that history teaches. Your acquisition of an understanding of what to look for and what items have the most importance in historical studies will render survey history courses more meaningful.

Table of Contents

A Definition of History

1

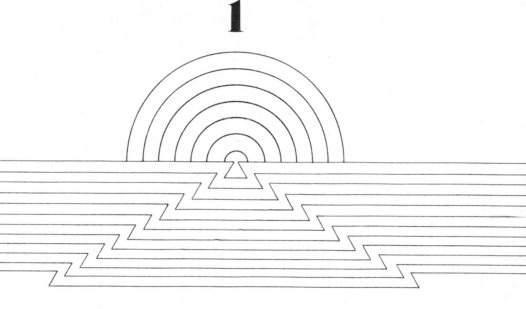

Historians are not at all agreed on an exact definition of their discipline. The field is so complex that it is almost impossible to obtain anything approaching a consensus. However, the definition presented below does provide a basis for classroom discussion and argument.

In its broadest and most elementary sense, history could be defined as a record of the past. But this would not really constitute a working definition. For one point, the definition would be overly simplified. For another, it would suggest an extremely formidable and ambitious, yet at the same time nebulous, task for the historian.

Our introductory definition would suggest that history is concerned with a tremendously long span of time. Actually this is not the case. History is concerned with a very minute portion of the lifetime of the earth. Geologists have informed us that the earth is somewhere between three and four billion years old. People, in their most primitive form, are estimated to have walked the face of the earth for something on the order of roughly 3,000,000 years.[1] History is concerned with a record of the past insofar as it applies to human beings. So if we choose to be charitable and refer to the earliest hominid as a human being, we have narrowed our original broad definition to cover approximately 1/200th of the period during which our planet is reputed to have existed. We happily leave the rest to the geologist.[2]

Hence, our definition should read that history is a record of the *human* past. The word "record" should be emphasized also, for by emphasizing that, history can be limited to an even smaller time period than that dating from the early hominid forms. People have left written records for roughly five thousand years. And it is these five thousand years of written records that concern the discipline of history. Leaving earlier man to the study of the anthropologist and archaeologist, but not by any means ignoring their findings, the historian is actually concerned with only 1/750,000th of the lifetime of our planet, for this is the time span of "civilized" human existence.

Although this is an infinitesimal period by geological standards, it provides no end of problems for practicing historians. It also provides, however, a more exact definition of history: History is a record of the human past from the point when written records began to appear. History is the record of what we might loosely term "human civilization" as far as we are able to ascertain it.

So historians record the facts of human existence, and this is still a very formidable and ambitious task—even for such a relatively short span of time. But historians perform two other functions as well, both of which must be included in any thorough definition of the discipline. Historians must interpret facts in an orderly and intelligible manner. They must also attempt to discover patterns and trends, or make generalizations that explain the behavior of people and nations throughout recorded time. If historians did not attempt to perform these two all-important functions, they would become nothing more than mere chroniclers—diary keepers—and consequently the pages of human history would read just like an accountant's ledger and be just about as interesting.

---

[1] See Melvin M. Payne, "Preserving the Treasures of Olduvai Gorge," *National Geographic,* Vol. 130, No. 5 (November 1966). The article pertains to the discovery by the late Louis Leakey of *Homo habilis,* a form estimated to be almost two million years old. See also R. E. F. Leakey, "Evidence for an Advanced Plio-Pleistocene Hominid from East Rudolph, Kenya," *Nature,* Vol. 242, No. 5398 (April 13, 1973); in 1972 Louis Leakey's son, Richard, unearthed a skull near Lake Rudolph, which he discusses in this article. The skull, labeled KNM-ER 1470, is dated at 2.6 million years.

[2] See Appendix B for a chart showing the relative time spans of geological history and "human" history.

Historians are constantly searching for basic factors or principles of human existence. For those bygone human events that they uncover, historians seek to discover underlying causes and meanings. They must continually search for the answer as to why something happened, trying to piece together the fragments of the past in order to understand it better and, in some instances, to gain better insight into developments that occurred in later periods. In a sense, due to the fact that they are seeking a basic understanding of human events, behavior, and existence, historians are in some measure philosophers, for they are concerned with the underlying scheme or pattern of human activities. Although the historians' philosophy is used to order and interpret the bits of evidence that make up the past, it is not a philosophy that resides solely within the realm of ideas; it rests on some concrete facts—historical evidence. The noted European historian, Johan Huizinga, has very ably emphasized this concept, positing that history is an intellectual activity, but one which is very much grounded in fact and reality.[3] Hence historians "philosophize" the past in order to explain it more satisfactorily. Some historians gain further understanding by comparing interpretations of history in light of changing attitudes or new evidence.

We have now arrived at the point where we can further clarify our original definition: History is the interpretive study of the recorded facts of bygone individuals and societies, undertaken to develop an understanding of human actions, not only in the past but in the present as well.

Such was not always the case. History in its present form is a fairly young field of study.[4] It developed as a distinct field during the eighteenth and nineteenth centuries, a direct result of the liberating influence of the writings of philosophical giants in the seventeenth century. The newly recognized field of history reflected their philosophical beliefs. Prior to that time history was a branch of grammar in the medieval Trivium—part of the classical curriculum of the Carolingian Palace School over a thousand years ago.

---

[3] Johan Huizinga, "A Definition of the Concept of History," *Philosophy and History: Essays Presented to Ernst Cassirer,* eds. Raymond Klibansky and H. J. Paton (New York: Harper & Row, Publishers, 1963). This particular essay is recommended to all students of history.

[4] Historians are not agreed on the exact time when history, in a modern sense, had its beginnings. One of the widely regarded "founders" of the discipline is Jean Bodin, whose *Methodus ad Facilem Historiarum Cognitionem (Method for the Easy Comprehension of History)* was published in 1566. Prominent at the present time is the name of Ibn Khaldun, an Arab historian, whose *Muqaddimah (Introduction)* (the first part of a larger work entitled *Kitab al-'Ibar* or *Book of Examples*) dates from the fourteenth century.

Writing at a time when people were first beginning to discover the various laws that explain the physical world, the philosophers of the Enlightenment reflected the prevailing optimism of their age. Heretofore unknown laws of the natural order were now discovered; why could there not also be various laws that govern human behavior with equal validity? Going one step further, these philosophers assumed that such laws did in fact exist, and that it was the purpose of the historian to discover them.[5]

Seeking a justification for their new discipline, a few advocates of history looked forward to the day when history would develop into a pure science. Some historians believed that they would eventually discover laws explaining humanity that would have the same force and validity as those laws governing the physical world. Science was king. Hence, the historian, in an attempt to give his discipline status, mistakenly referred to it as a "science."

The viewpoint implicit in the label "science" is totally incorrect. Science deals with materials that can be—directly or indirectly—touched, weighed, measured, and evaluated under laboratory conditions. Science deals with concrete, verifiable objects. History, on the other hand, does not deal with materials that can be touched, weighed, and measured. History is inferential, i.e., it infers the past on the basis of partially known facts. True, historians make use of some concrete materials in their work, such as documents, diaries, newspapers, and contemporary accounts, but from these they must infer the rest. Historians can never know the past with complete certainty. They can never formulate laws as determinate as scientific laws of the physical universe.

Those who attempted to make of history a pure science according to the prevailing notions of the Enlightenment would have in effect made science their god.[6] According to this belief, anything that was not totally scientific was of an inferior order. But the position was at best a tenuous one. The scientific method applies to the sciences—to physics, chemistry, and biology. It does not apply to people in their social context. Science may affect and influence individuals extrinsically, but science has nothing to offer individuals in developing their humanity. The so-called social sciences and the exact sciences are different disciplinary areas. Their subject matter is entirely different, and their methodology is par-

[5] An excellent brief essay on the significance of the Enlightenment on the development of history as a separate discipline is found in Patrick Gardiner, *Theories of History* (Glencoe, Illinois: The Free Press, 1959), Author's Introduction to the work.

[6] The attempt of some early historians to liken themselves to pure scientists is very capably denounced in Jose Ortega y Gasset, *History As a System: And Other Essays Toward a Philosophy of History* (New York: W. W. Norton & Company, Inc., 1961). See particularly "History as a System."

tially different. One is not better than the other; they operate in separate spheres. Not being of the same order, they cannot be compared.

Historians do make use of scientific methodology up to a point. They gather the facts, organize the facts, and draw conclusions from those facts. They make hypotheses on the basis of whatever facts are definitely known. This is also what scientists do. But historians are unable to verify hypotheses by experimentation; they cannot replay an event in a laboratory setting—a very significant final step of the scientific method. Hence, they are not true scientists. They are primarily philosophers. So to our most recent definition of history, we must add the salient point that history is a humanistic discipline, the study of human nature and human affairs as best they can be observed.

Although it does not alter the classification of history as a distinct discipline, it should be pointed out that in certain instances historical researchers do make some use of the tools of the exact sciences for such purposes as determining the authenticity of old documents and ascertaining the age of a document by means of paper, water mark, or ink analysis. This is strictly a laboratory technique that aids historians in collecting facts and determining their reliability. But science is of no direct help to historians in the performance of their primary function, which is to interpret—to discover or formulate laws, patterns, and trends in an attempt to explain human behavior and events.

Historians make no claim that history provides solutions for problems; historians attempt to identify problems and to point out when, why, and how they occurred. Historians study the human past, a rather mysterious and confusing conglomeration of apparently disordered facts that seem to bear contingent relationships to one another (some historians have adopted this viewpoint). Historians are concerned with people throughout recorded time and with human nature. They must always make provision for the motivation of historical events.

Thus, historians cannot be strict determinists—i.e., they cannot hold that an inflexible set of environmental factors inexorably determine human behavior—and still be able to perform their function. For strict determinists there would be no value in studying human behavior in the past because it could not ever be altered: People would be incapable of learning from their past errors.

In addition, historians cannot permit themselves the mistake of isolating a particular person or event. Human events do not occur in a vacuum; and because this is the case, they affect individuals and, in turn, other events. Consequently, all historical occurrences must be considered from a broad perspective.

Finally, historians must be in positions to render solid value judgments concerning the behavior of the historical subjects they are considering. Otherwise, by failing to determine the long-range significance of an event and only illuminating its importance at the time of its immediate occurrence, they will leave an important aspect of their task undone.

In its historical development history at one time either provided data for or embraced all other disciplines. Etymologically, the Greek word *historia* meant "inquiry" or the knowledge acquired from inquiry. Early histories were often compendia of known facts; for example, Aristotle's *History of Animals* attempted to survey natural life by classifying the properties and functions of animals, and Pliny the Elder's *Natural Histories* was actually an encyclopaedia of information known at the time concerning all the arts and sciences. In its broadest sense, history evolved as knowledge of concrete, particular things and thus encompassed all knowledge, and it has at various times been identified with philosophy, physical and biological science, social science, the arts, and, quite importantly, with the history of history itself. The growth of knowledge and its subsequent compartmentalization has led to a tendency to narrow individual fields of inquiry. Historians, in order to perform fully their interpretive functions, cannot repudiate the original broad application of the word *historia*.

Historians seek to understand the human past in an effort to better understand an ever changing present, with the ambitious hope that such an understanding will provide worthwhile guidelines for the future. The greater the knowledge possessed by historians of all facets of human behavior, the greater should be their understanding of the events they are attempting to evaluate. Consequently, truly competent historians must necessarily possess a working knowledge of psychology, philosophy, sociology, political science, economics, and some sort of a moral or theological system. True historians, to borrow the terminology of the medical profession, are not specialists; they are general practitioners. They cannot compartmentalize the various areas of human knowledge and behavior that apply to people as people. They cannot fragment human existence. If they are going to adequately explain past human activities, they must be knowledgeable in all disciplines that are concerned with human behavior. They may, however, emphasize the role of one or more of these disciplines in shaping human behavior. But historians must be equipped to integrate the various artificial divisions of human knowledge.

Professional historians are also detectives—but detectives by remote control. They must know how to use clues (documents) in order to reconstruct the story of the human race, just as detectives seek out and utilize clues in an attempt to reconstruct a crime. But historical reconstruction is on a far more grandiose scale; it must take into account many more variables, and it possesses the added complexity of pertaining to actions which took place hundreds or perhaps thousands of years in the past.

As a result of these difficulties, historians must exercise a tremendous degree of precision and care in selecting and organizing documents.[7] A tiny slip could be compounded over centuries into an error of great magnitude. Historians must also look for the motivation for whatever they are investigating. This is their interpretation of events. However, it cannot be held with complete certitude. The past undoubtedly shapes the present; for example, historians agree that the terms of the Treaty of Versailles made possible a climate wherein Nazi Germany could develop. But the present, through its interpretation of the past, shapes the past also, at least in terms of the present's understanding of the past. Historians are creatures of their own time and culture. Even with a superhuman effort at complete detachment, they cannot help but subconsciously "adjust" the past somewhat to meet their own personal standards and convictions. This is where broad knowledge of human nature must enter the picture and influence thinking. The greater the knowledge possessed by historians, the greater should be their degree of successfully attained objectivity in determining the past, and consequently the greater should be the accuracy of their interpretation of the past.

Having reconstructed and interpreted the past with some degree of accuracy, the task of historians is not yet completed. Historians must next consider past events in terms of their effects on later developments in order to give them proper significance. And if they so desire, historians may then attempt to identify some trends in human events based on their understanding of the facts.

Historians are always looking for trends in human activities. But even if historians identify a trend with complete certitude, this does not preclude the possibility that the trend will halt at any particular future moment. In fact, by the very fact that historians do identify a trend, they may make possible the climate of opinion that will divert or destroy that trend. For example, American participation in the United Nations was in large measure based on an avoidance of the conditions which had led to American

[7] An excellent advanced work is Gilbert J. Garraghan, *A Guide to Historical Method*, ed. Jean Delanglez (New York: Fordham University Press, 1946). More useful to the beginning student would be the appropriate chapters in Allan Nevins, *Gateway to History* (rev. ed.; Boston: D. C. Heath Company, 1962).

repudiation of participation in the League of Nations following World War I.

Historians are always seeking the causes of various effects. For instance, like everyone else, they know that wars occur. But historians hope to discover *why* they exist. They want to be able to state that when certain conditions are present, a war is a distinct possibility. Again, they will never be able to reduce causes to mathematical formulae. But their effort to discover the *why* of things is the real merit and worth of history.

Historians make no claims that history can provide the answers for a better human existence, but they at least make an attempt to find the answers if they do exist. Historians wisely do not guarantee that mistakes will not be repeated in the future, but they do point out those mistakes that have been made and repeated in the past.

History has a rich and varied tradition. It is because of this richness and variety that historians have been assigned a myriad of tasks to perform. The purposes of historical study include "general education," awareness of past experiences of the human race, the demonstration of what is true, the unification of all knowledge, and the uncovery of data for use in other disciplines. On another level, historical inquiry has been credited with seeking patterns to guide future development, providing past examples for future emulation or avoidance, providing cures for present ills by uncovering past causes, and discovering transcendental values that bind the human race. Thus, historians may take on many roles. In addition to their popularly regarded roles as scholars and teachers, they may be philosophers, scientists, futurists, theologians, politicians, journalists, and behaviorists.

Just as there are many roles for the historian, so too there are many definitions of history. But we offer the following basic definition as a guide for the beginning student:

> History is the humanistic, interpretive study of past human society, the purpose of which is to gain insight into the present with the fervent hope of perhaps influencing a more favorable future.

Questions for Discussion

1. What are the purposes of historical study? Discuss the strengths and weaknesses of history as a "science" and history as a "craft."

2. Compare and contrast various definitions of history. Evaluate their validity in terms of your own definition of history.

3. Account for the identification of history with such varied disciplines as science, philosophy, and the arts.

4. Is history deterministic? To what degree does chance play a role in human affairs?

5. Enumerate and evaluate the problems associated with the historian's interpretation of historical events. Is objectivity possible in historical inquiry?

Problems in the
Study of History
2

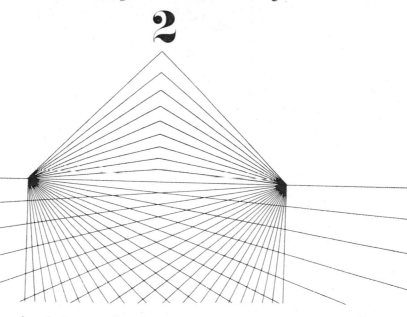

It has already been pointed out that history at the introductory survey course level is too frequently regarded as a memorization course in names, dates, and events. This attitude quite obviously reflects neither the purpose nor the function of the discipline of history. The names, dates, and events of history are nothing more than tools employed by historians to serve an end, just as the hammer and saw are the tools of carpenters or mathematical knowledge is a tool of research scientists.

Historians must use historical fact in order to gain some understanding of the present if they hope to obtain some insight into the future. The same is true of students in a history course. The facts of history provide the necessary foundation stones for a real inquiry into human nature. With this in mind, the problems that beginning college students of history will encounter are presented below.

1. Cause-and-Effect Relationships

One of the most difficult problems encountered in the study of history concerns how to accurately assess the causes for various historical occurrences. A proper study of history should result in an awareness of how attitudes, ideas, and events flow and develop throughout recorded time. Historians attempt to discover the causes or reasons for these attitudes, ideas, and events. They inquire into their interrelationship.

It is hardly sufficient to state that, because the battleship *Maine* was blown up in Cuba shortly before the Spanish-American War erupted, the *Maine* disaster was responsible for the ensuing conflict. The disaster did constitute an immediate, prior event, but this alone did not necessarily make it a cause for the war.[1]

Historians must search out real and substantiated causes; they cannot content themselves with using immediate, prior incidents to explain subsequent events.[2] No doubt there were causes for the Spanish-American War; and historians must determine what these causes were. They fully recognize that there was no single isolated cause or simple explanation for any of the complex events of history. Life is not that simple.

As matters turn out, the sinking of the battleship *Maine* was a factor in bringing about the war. After delving deeper into the background of the war, historians soon discovered that whether or not the Spanish authorities in Cuba actually sank the vessel is irrelevant (it is still unknown) as a causal factor. The American public jumped to the conclusion that Spain was guilty of sinking the vessel, and anti-Spanish sentiment increased in the nation. Historians, then, have to analyze the reasons why Americans were so willing to accept the sinking of the *Maine* as justification for seeking war with Spain. And with this intent historians discover such factors as the "yellow press," McKinley's bowing to vested interests, and the resurrection of the Black Legend (stories of inherent Spanish cruelty, particularly in dealing with non-Christians)—all of which aid in explaining the war temper of the American people.

Behind the obvious, there are causes for the Spanish-American War—and for all other historical events as well—that must be sought out just as detectives build up clues piecemeal in reconstructing a crime. Some causes may be remote; they may superficially appear unrelated. But causes can never be ignored simply because they are not obvious. Nor should the extension of causal factors into the past imply that we should blame every human mishap on

---

[1] This distinction between real and immediate causes was first emphasized by Thucydides during the fifth century B.C. It remains a major concern for historians today.

[2] The beginning student may desire to probe more deeply into the various aspects of "cause" and "effect." Any good logic text would provide such materials. By way of example, see Irving M. Copi, *Introduction to Logic* (2nd ed.; New York: The Macmillan Company, 1961), especially Chapter XII.

the biblical fact that Adam ate the forbidden fruit. While it is true that historians seek out both direct and indirect causes, they do not trace events back to Adam's fall and the concept of original sin and thereby evade assigning responsibility for historical events.

Causes are exceedingly difficult to assess. Historians must be very careful to avoid an over-reliance on convenient, but not necessarily adequate, explanations. Every human event is complex; a multitude of forces, some known and others unknown, shape and influence it. But this does not mean that every explanation of a human event should be cluttered with reams of trivial data.

To get to the heart of the matter, cause-and-effect relationships pertain to nothing more than plain, basic, logical method. Both professional historians and survey course history students must be able to think logically and systematically if they hope to derive full benefit from the discipline of history. However, it should be noted that by the very fact that history cannot be classified as a laboratory science (as discussed in Chapter 1), there may be various logical, valid interpretations of the same historical event. The problem of historians is to find the interpretation which best accords with the generally accepted, factual information available —there may, of course, be more than one interpretation.

Having determined the causes for a historical event, historians must then determine the effects of the event. By definition a cause is anything producing an effect. And, since the threads of human experience are intertwined, effects, in turn, become causes for other effects. This fact emphasizes all the more the interpretive nature of historical inquiry.

One of the generally accepted causes for poverty is lack of opportunity. Poverty is, among other things, an effect of lack of opportunity. But poverty is also the cause of other effects—social unrest, welfare programs, and so forth. Historians must ascertain the effects as well as the causes of historical events if a proper understanding of those events is to be achieved.

The accounts of historians depend upon a number of considerations, all of which are valid if logically pursued:

1.   The availability of facts concerning an event will affect the interpretation of that event; as more information becomes available, new interpretations will be formulated.
2.   The personal interests and perspectives of historians individualize their accounts of historical events.
3.   The circumstances and values of the time when historians write affect their interpretations; historians writing about a nation with which their country is at war will probably give a different portrayal than they would if that nation were an ally.

4.   All historians possess a philosophy (their assumptions and methods) which provides the basis for their interpretation of history and their structuring of historical events.

5.   There are various modes of incomplete evidence, ranging from lack of documents to misinterpreted documents to disregarded documents, all of which affect the account of a historical event.

The reconstruction of a historical event is analogous to the working of a jigsaw puzzle which has a number of different pieces which fit the same key opening. All the pieces must be tried and viewed against the entire puzzle to determine the best "fit."

2.   Time Perspective

Students of history must also be cognizant of the significance of time and the problems associated with it, both in span and in chronology.[3] It is not possible to adequately conceptualize the vast immensity of time, but an honest effort is a necessary prerequisite for the development of historical mindedness. An appreciation of time sequence is imperative for a thorough understanding of cause and effect relationships. Hence, dates become important tools for students of history.

The placing of events in proper sequential order is normally far more important than the exact dates of the events themselves. The degree of exactitude of the date of any event depends upon the circumstances surrounding it. For instance, the month and the day of the year 800 A.D. when Charlemagne was crowned emperor by the Pope is relatively unimportant. The fact that the event took place on Christmas Day is perhaps interesting and reflective of the medieval religious spirit but not really essential. The month of the year 1588 when the Spanish Armada set sail for England is very important, because knowledge of the season during which the Armada sailed has a bearing on an understanding of the tremendous losses which the Spaniards incurred due to seasonal storms in the North Sea. During the kaleidoscopic events in France in 1789, exact days of the month are extremely important in order to determine the causal relationship among numerous closely occurring events. And in an event like the Japanese attack on Pearl Harbor where historians wish to fix responsibility for the lack of American

---

[3]Chronological tables are often useful tools for survey course students. They enable them to grasp the idea of time perspective. Incidentally, the formulation of such tables by students is often a good study technique. See Appendix B for chronological tables of the Western world.

defenses, it may be necessary to study the day hour by hour. Again, this minuteness of study would depend on the nature of the historical inquiry.

Then, too, the circumstances surrounding the event under consideration will usually determine the minuteness to be observed in placing it within a given time period. The pre-Cambrian period would be dated in terms of millions of years, but to state that Columbus discovered America within the past million years would be entirely devoid of meaning. Mature judgment should prevail when considering the degree of exactitude for dates, but chronology—the order of events—must be strictly observed under all circumstances.

3. Objectivity and Tolerance

One of the most important functions of historical inquiry and one of the greatest difficulties in the study of history concerns objectivity and tolerance. Objectivity means the use of historical facts without personal bias or prejudice. Tolerance means giving a full and impartial hearing to an opposing view and respecting that view, provided it is derived honestly.

Objective historians must respect the opinions of their peers, provided, of course, that these opinions are methodically formulated, even though the historians might wholeheartedly and vigorously disagree with these opinions from a strictly personal viewpoint. Such an attitude implies an at least tacit acceptance of tolerance. Couple this tolerance with an honest attempt toward objectivity (realizing, of course, that no human being is capable of complete objectivity—a decided but unavoidable drawback to the discipline), and history, perhaps, is in the position to make the greatest contribution among all fields of human knowledge to the general education of an individual. It is not the acquisition of historical fact, but rather the acceptance of the historical technique that can bring about this general education. Unfortunately, in the survey history course it is more often historical fact than historical technique that is taught. Nonetheless, an individual thoroughly grounded in the proper study of history is capable of doing much to lessen the amount of bigotry and prejudice in the world.

Students should be cautioned, however, against accepting too readily any historical interpretation, regardless of its claims toward objectivity. No matter how intellectually honest historians might be, whatever they write is the product of their own environment, education, and value structure. Their interpretations are the results of their personal beliefs and outlook on life. It is impossible for

these influences not to affect their writings.[4] Some of the most
sincere individuals who have taken up the writing of history have
been the most incorrect. Unfortunately the historical technique
can very readily be employed as a two-edged sword, capable of
defending bigotry and prejudice as well as cutting them down. A
close scrutiny of the historian's presuppositions, criteria, and principles is necessary to prevent the arbitrary intrusion of prejudice.

There are certain problems attendant even to the proper utilization of history. Every generation and every culture has its own
opinion as to what worth and importance should be attached to
the past (this is very interestingly brought out in George Orwell's
1984). It depends entirely on prevailing values and moral structure. History is always interpreted by the present. Obviously, then,
the nature of the present will determine one's understanding of the
past. A pagan present would afford one picture of human history,
whereas a present highly imbued with Judeo-Christian beliefs
would portray a completely different picture. Both cultures would
be utilizing the same canvas and the same paint, but the brush
strokes would differ. Yet within their respective contexts, both
these societies could create their own objective versions of the
past. And necessarily, the end results of their studies would not
represent the same human fabric.

Truth *can change* in history. What is accepted as true at one
time may be superseded by the discovery of new evidence, reinterpretation, or the presence of a different milieu at another time.
And truth may change even in the absence of any attempt to
deceive or to consciously slant history on the part of the historian.

If honestly attempted objective history suffers from serious
drawbacks, one can readily imagine the degree of difficulty associated with the use of history for nonobjective purposes. Historical
writings can be propagandized; and it cannot be stressed too greatly that deliberately propagandized history is really not history
at all.

The facts can be presented accurately in a historical account,
but the account can still be slanted. One manner is to omit a fact
or a body of facts from an account. This particular technique has
been used quite consistently, though generally unconsciously, in
the general exclusion of minority group and female contributions

[4] The following works contain useful accounts of this difficulty: J. Huizinga, "A
Definition of the Concept of History," *Philosophy and History: Essays Presented to
Ernst Cassirer*, eds. Raymond Klibansky and H. J. Paton (New York: Harper & Row,
Publishers, 1963), Patrick Gardiner, *Theories of History* (Glencoe, Illinois: The Free
Press, 1959), especially pp. 344-355, and Herbert Muller, *The Uses of the Past: Profiles
of Former Societies* (New York: Oxford University Press, 1957).

to various aspects of history (see Chapter 7). Historians are usually not deliberate in such omissions; the omissions result from environmental, traditional, and habitual influences on writers of history. Similarly, word choice may introduce a bias to otherwise accurately presented historical data. The use of the term "massacre" to describe a successful Indian military venture, while the word "victory" is used to describe a successful U.S. Cavalry venture, predisposes readers to regard Indians as savages. Finally, the injection of nationalism and/or patriotism into historical writing can create an unbalanced depiction—i.e., the accounts of various U.S. historians reporting on our wars with various other nations.

Nevertheless, a very serious difficulty presents itself; and it is compounded by the fact that there is a fine dividing line between an erroneous interpretation or an unintentional error in methodology on the one hand, and a deliberate attempt to propagandize under the guise of historical objectivity on the other hand. The effects on the reader would be equally damaging in either case. Both professional historians and students of history must be constantly on guard against the danger of unreliable materials, interpretations, and conclusions.

4. Philosophy of History

Historians, if they are going to be something other than mere compilers of unrelated fact, must concern themselves with formulating a direction or general course of human events and developments. They must conduct a conscientious and legitimate search for meaning in history. And history students, if they are going to become something other than mere memorizers of meaningless, confused fact, must be fully aware of this concern and this search and appreciate its value.

Practicing historians, of course, must always be careful not to formulate patterns to the point of overgeneralization (even though some generalization is necessary in the study of history).[5] When historians posit generalizations both they and students of history must accept those generalizations for what they are: They do not apply to every set of circumstances; they may not even provide a complete explanation for the items under consideration. Historians are incapable of tying human affairs into neat little packages (even though they must occasionally fight the tendency to do so), for

---

[5] See Louis Gottschalk (ed.), *Generalization in the Writing of History* (Chicago: The University of Chicago Press, 1963), for an introduction to the immense complexity of this problem.

they are dealing with a constantly changing story, an unpredictable human will, and enormous gaps in their own knowledge.

Nor should historians deceive themselves by claiming the ability to predict the future (occasionally one succumbs to the temptation). Historians are not soothsayers; they do not possess crystal balls. But they are able to make some reasonably reliable estimates concerning the course of present events, in light of past developments, and in this manner they can shed some possible light on the future. Thus, philosophy of history is an attempt to organize and account for the human past in such a manner that it becomes meaningful and worthwhile.

The philosophy of history, in its origin, development, and scope, will be developed more fully in the next chapter. But at this point it should be indicated that there are a few concepts which must be adhered to by both the historian and the student of history if they are to develop a meaningful philosophy of history. For example, it seems that the concept of the solidarity of the human race is a *sine qua non*. All people in all ages, regardless of location or stage of civilization, have some effect on one another. They are all members of the human family, and there is a certain unity in the human experience. Another example is the acceptance of a value system, a subject that is considered in the following section.

5. A Value System

Human beings have their own personal outlooks on life, which are based on their education, their environment, and their experiences. Their understanding of what has preceded them is conditioned by these outlooks. Consequently the discipline of history must be considered in the light of some sort of a value system, and that value system is determined by the culture in which historians live. To render any sort of a judgment means to compare an action against an already accepted mode of behavior. This does not mean that an interpretation of history must reflect only one particular theological system, but rather that it is almost bound to reflect a moral, humanistic, esthetic set of principles based upon the cumulative contributions of Western civilization operating within the framework of the Judeo-Christian tradition. For such is the heritage of Western people and the generally accepted value structure of the Western world. This does not, of course, preclude historians who uphold a different value structure from writing history from their own non-Western frame of reference, e.g., doctrinaire Marxists.

American students would find a history of their country written by an Indian Buddhist peculiar in its approach and alien in its judgments, while adherents to Buddhism would not. The reader of history must be able to identify with, or at least be knowledgeable about, the value structure utilized by the historian in order to profit from his or her study. Furthermore, it would not be very meaningful for an American historian to interpret the history of Pomerania in terms of the value structure of the American Great Awakening. We have our own cultural heritage that must be employed to properly interpret and to properly understand ourselves. We must interpret the conduct of others, as far as is humanly possible, first by their own standards; having done that, we can compare them with our own or other standards. Similarly, non-Americans should interpret us first by our standards, and then compare us with their own. This approach in no way restricts the activities of historians operating within their own value system; this is the only approach they can use if they are to properly perform their function. It should be pointed out, however, that some cultural frameworks are more restrictive than others; thus, under certain conditions the interpretive function of certain historians is limited.

We have been suggesting that there are certain widely held values that are peculiar to the Judeo-Christian tradition of Western civilization—the framework in which an overwhelming majority of Americans are currently operating. These values are relatively simple to ascertain. They include the concepts of human dignity and the right to life (currently undergoing examination in face of the abortion drive), a recognition of both good and evil in the world and the fundamental opposition between these two forces, and the fact that with every claimed right or privilege there are corresponding obligations.

All of the concepts mentioned above and many more reflect the absolute necessity of a solidly grounded value structure for the success of any human endeavor. The historian can neither explain nor interpret history without possessing a value system. An accepted frame of reference is necessary before the rendering of judgments can even take place. How can we possibly claim that a given action is good or bad unless we first have some idea of what the words "good" and "bad" signify? How can we possibly claim that something is true or false unless we first have some idea of what the words "true" and "false" signify? Our only alternative would be to claim amorality, and then we would only succeed in plunging the discipline backwards into a meaningless void.

There is one very serious difficulty arising out of the value system concept. As has already been indicated, historians are prone to interpret past events of their own social and cultural structure. This is most proper and commendable for purposes of comparison, but it cannot, under any circumstances, be utilized as an evaluative norm. Otherwise we would lose the flavor of the past. Nor can the knowledge of the present be used in assessing causes for past events. It is rather easy to be a Sunday morning quarterback, since all facts are then known. Causes as we see them are not necessarily causes as the past saw them. As far as possible, bygone people must be interpreted in terms of their own, not the interpreting historian's, value structure. Afterward, conclusions may be drawn by comparison with the historian's own value structure. Only by evaluating the achievements and failures of human beings according to the acceptable standards of the time when those achievements and failures actually took place can the historian hope to acquire some understanding of these standards for the present day. Again, a plea is being made for tolerance, for this is a legitimate function of history.

6. A Unique Discipline

History possesses a unique role as a discipline primarily because it is a very encompassing discipline. It is not strictly a social science or a behavioral science or one of the humanities, and it is definitely not an exact science. Yet it combines elements of these areas of knowledge in one complex, integrated package. Consequently history provides an excellent mechanism for broadly educating an individual in that it aptly demonstrates the correlation and integration of all branches of human knowledge. It could not be otherwise, for history is concerned with the study of man in all his endeavors. If individuals are ever to realize the ancient maxim "Know Thyself," they must begin by studying human life in its totality.

The unique role of history as an encompassing discipline is exceedingly important in an age when bodies of human knowledge are continually being fragmented and compartmentalized owing to the tremendous growth of knowledge over the past few centuries. History is capable of providing a trunk line for all human knowledge. Within its framework, any and every discipline can and should be considered.

Some remarkable progress has been made along these lines in recent years, e.g., American Studies programs, History of Ideas programs, and History of Science programs, plus a host of integrated approaches. These innovative programs comprise an ambitious task for history, but history is a rather ambitious discipline. It provides the basis for understanding the structure and development of the total human being.

Of course the uniqueness of history as a discipline creates some rather serious problems for students in an introductory survey course, in that they generally do not yet possess a wide range of knowledge to integrate. But over a few short years the knowledge they do have will grow tremendously. Lower division history students should begin their task of acquiring a complete, integrated education as quickly as possible. The longer it is put off, the more difficult it will become.

Becoming a veritable storehouse of encyclopedic knowledge, of course, is not the same thing as becoming an educated individual. One of the principal characteristics of truly educated people is their ability to integrate and correlate knowledge. Educated people possess a broad and tolerant view of life. Since they cannot obtain this broad perspective by specializing in a single, isolated discipline, they turn to history for a total picture of humanity.

Questions for Discussion

1.   Discuss some of the techniques of substantiation for an interpretation of a given historical event.

2.   In what respects can history be classified as an art? As a science? As a social science? As a kind of philosophy?

3.   Discuss some of the elements that hinder objectivity in the selection and interpretation of historical evidence.

4.   How can you account for the fact that truth *changes* in history? What are the implications of this fact for the study of history?

5.   How does one go about assessing causes for historical events? How can the accuracy of causes be ascertained?

Philosophies of History

3

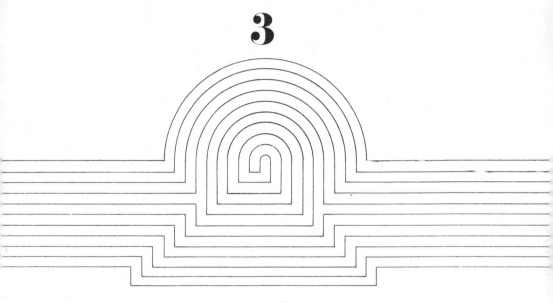

The term "philosophy of history" pertains to that particular branch of historical study which places major emphasis on the ultimate course of human civilization. A philosophy of history is the personal interpretation and judgment of the individual who is formulating it; it is his or her set of assumptions for ordering the course of historical facts.[1] It attempts to systematize the vast bulk of fact comprising the human past, and in the process it gives meaning to the human experience.

Since its validity resides only in the minds of its formulator and those individuals who choose to accept it, a philosophy of history cannot be verified any more than the pure philosophical systems of such great thinkers as Descartes, Locke, and Kant can. Nevertheless, a philosophy of history, if logically formulated, poses considerable food for thought. And, occasionally, a particular philosophy of history can exert a tremendous influence on the shaping of the world, e.g., the theory of dialectical materialism formulated by Karl Marx.

[1] For a detailed consideration of this topic, see Richard McKeon, "Truth and the History of Ideas," *Thought, Action and Passion* (Chicago: The University of Chicago Press, 1954), pp. 54-88.

Students of history should possess a fundamental knowledge of the various major interpretations of history. The purpose of this chapter is to provide that knowledge in outline form so that the beginning student of history will be in a better position both to consider history in its true perspective and to understand the justification for history as a discipline. It is further hoped that students will become equipped to intelligently choose, develop, or adapt their own philosophy of history more discriminately.

1. The Cyclical View

The first widespread interpretation of history was the cyclical theory. In Western culture the cyclical theory existed in dominant form from the time of Herodotus (484-425 B.C.) to the time of Christ.[2] According to the cyclical viewpoint all human events occur in cycles. Names, dates, and persons may change, but periodically what happened before will happen again and for the same reasons. This applies equally to nation-states and to epochs. We have all heard the trite statement that history repeats itself. Those who make such a statement, whether they realize it or not, are reflecting the cyclical theory.

Cyclicalism standing alone is not a philosophy of history in the true meaning of the term. A philosophy of history presupposes a beginning, middle course, and end or realization for the human experience. A repeating cycle is meaningless; it has no realization. It is merely proceeding to its own beginning. But when combined with various other notions, the cyclical idea could and did result in some rather interesting and influential philosophies of history.

The cyclical theory was predominant in the ancient world when people possessed no real knowledge of the universe or the role that they were destined to play in it. In that period everything but the immediate present was relatively insignificant. The theorists of the ancient world made the first small steps in the area of philosophy of history which were ultimately destined to give rise to a fruitful field of inquiry.

The cyclical theory made no real contribution to man's knowledge concerning his role in this life. The importance of the cyclical theory lies in the fact that it was the first known theory of history,

---

[2] This does not imply that there are no longer any cyclical historians. Oswald Spengler and Arnold Toynbee are both members of the school. Also, I am excluding any consideration of cyclical theories in Eastern thought; in the East cyclicalism has traditionally enjoyed more widespread acceptance than in the West. An excellent work, tracing cyclicalism historically in both East and West, is Grace Cairns, *Philosophies of History: Meeting of East and West in Cycle-Pattern Theories of History* (New York: Philosophical Library, Inc., 1962).

later synthesized with other concepts. But along came Christianity, and the Christians of Europe experienced a considerable amount of difficulty in interpreting the Messianic promise in terms of the cyclical theory. Christians regarded the coming of Christ as a unique event. His coming was not something that would be repeated every two, three, or four hundred years; for if it would repeat itself periodically, it would become commonplace and thereby lose much of its significance. Thus, the cyclical theory witnessed a rather abrupt setback in Western thought as the dominant historical pattern. In altered form it remains to the present day, but it has been tempered considerably by combination with other ideas.

2. The Providential View

After the influence of the cyclical theory declined, the next dominant interpretation in Europe was the providential view of history. The view had existed among certain peoples during the Old Testament era, notably the Hebrews, but it had been overshadowed by cyclicalism. The providential view was quite widespread during the church-oriented Middle Ages. Throughout this period every human and every natural occurrence was explained in terms of an intervening divine providence. Catastrophes, whether wars or earthquakes, were readily interpreted as divinely ordained punishment for some human wrongdoing. Peace and well-being were generally understood as signs that a divine providence was quite well satisfied with the activities of his creatures.

People, it appeared, had practically no control over their own environment, but this did not greatly disturb the "other world" mentality of the Middle Ages. For the providential viewpoint provided great security for a nonscientific people who possessed real knowledge neither of causation nor of the physical universe in which they were living. Medieval people did not believe it possible to exercise any control over their world.

One of the leading exponents and pioneers of the providential theory of history was Augustine of Hippo. A transitional figure, Augustine attempted to synthesize pagan cyclical thought and Greco-Roman intellectual achievements with the basic ideas of Christianity. The result of this attempt is a combination of cyclicalism and providence in history. Augustine's *De civitate Dei (The City of God)* is a philosophy of history. According to this work the world is made up of two symbolic cities: a city of good and a city of evil, representing God on the one side and the devil on the other. Human history consists of a recording of the struggle for ascendancy between these two opposing powers. The end of this struggle will be the final determination of either eternal salvation or eternal damnation for the entire human race.

People are relegated to the role of pawns in this game of high stakes. Quite naturally, they are deeply concerned about the outcome of the struggle, but they are extremely limited in doing anything about it. Obviously wanting the forces of good to win because of the promise of eternal happiness, they lead good lives in order to identify with their choice of combatants. But their world is strictly a battleground for eternity, and forces other than those under their control are shaping human destinies.

However, in this theory, human history has now achieved an end. The end is eternal salvation. For even though this end often appears quite uncertain—there would be battles won and battles lost by both the forces of good and evil—according to Augustine, God will win the struggle, and He will proceed to reward those human beings who have not lost faith in His abilities.

Within such a frame of reference, little or no heed was paid to material achievements. No material thing on the face of this earth was recognized as having any real importance. The earth was strictly a waiting room for eternity. Thus, the providential viewpoint was ideally suited for a spiritually oriented medieval Europe. It satisfied the existing cultural milieu—as all philosophies of history are prone to do. In terms of material or physical advancement for humanity the view is stagnant. This does not mean to imply that the Middle Ages witnessed no material advances. The unfortunate "Dark Ages" terminology does not do justice to the period. But material achievements often took a back seat in the existing value structure; and they often reflected the prevailing spiritualism, e.g., the erection of the famous medieval cathedrals.

Although the providential view of history has a diminishing influence in modern America, it was quite prevalent at one time. The Puritan ethic reflects a providential view. Calvinist teaching proclaimed the doctrine of the "elect," those people who were predestined to be saved; the sure sign of being one of the elect was to lead a saintly life. To this Calvinist notion, America added the concept that material success was a sign of divine favor. Not only was this new concept predicated on the belief that a divine providence directly intervened in human affairs, but it also provided the ideological basis for the growth of American capitalism. To this day the Puritan ethic is upheld by many Americans.

3.   The Progress View

With the birth of scientific interest and inquiry; the breakdown of institutionalized Christian unity; the rise of a materialistically minded middle class; and the discoveries of such great scientific minds as those of Newton, Leibnitz, and Galileo, Europe took on a new set of values. And out of this new set of values a new theory of history was formulated.

The cyclical theory had been superseded by the Christian providence view. Now that view came under attack because of the great advances taking place in the furtherance of human knowledge. Europe was becoming progressively more materialistic in outlook. It was becoming conscious of people as people. It was beginning to think that individuals might possibly have some control over their destiny and environment. It was discovering some of the secrets of the universe. Natural laws, not intervening providence, appeared to govern good and ill fortune. Europe was beginning to think in terms of improvements in daily human existence as well as of eternal salvation.

Around the beginning of the eighteenth century, the providential view was tempered somewhat by such thinkers as Bossuet and Vico, but it was left to the universal genius of Gottfried Leibnitz to introduce a new dominant historical theory. This new theory, which received widespread adoption by historians, was named the progress theory. According to its principal thesis, the human race is continually getting better and better. It is progressing, becoming more civilized with the passage of each new generation (or as Voltaire would put it, people are becoming more and more like Voltaire).[3]

The new theory of progress, imbued with the widespread optimism of the Age of the Enlightenment, placed complete faith in human rather than in divine abilities. It holds that each new generation builds upon the achievements of each preceding generation, and that as a result each new generation must be better (Leibnitz's law of continuity) because it has more with which to start. And this is a gradual, continual process; there are no halts, and there are no sudden surges of high achievement. The more rigid adherents of the theory quickly transformed this assumption into an inevitable law of nature. Individuals are required by nature to progress; no choice is had in the matter.

If, as the progress adherents hold, individuals are continually and inevitably progressing, the question immediately arises as to the ultimate end of this progress—if, indeed, such an end actually exists. Is it indefinite progress, or is there some definite goal to be

[3] An excellent work that traces the transition from providence to progress is John Bury, *The Idea of Progress* (London: Macmillan and Company, Ltd., 1921). There is no single work pertaining to the United States which covers the entire subject. However, an excellent work for the time period considered is Arthur A. Ekirch, *The Idea of Progress in America, 1815-1860* (New York: Peter Smith, 1951).

realized, either on earth or in eternity? By no means agreed on the answer to this question, the adherents of the progress viewpoint fragmented into various schools.

Some adherents posited indefinite progress strictly within the material realm; to these individuals progress was endless. Others predicted the eventual realization of a utopian society on earth, at which point progress would necessarily cease, for perfection would have been achieved. Still others believed that individuals would continually progress on earth but that there was an end to human history and that the real goal of the human race was to be found in eternity. Members of this latter group blended in a greater or lesser quantity of providence with their progress views, depending on their personal theological convictions. Regardless of the type of progress put forth, the idea of progress has become very much a part of our way of life in the twentieth century.

The progress view of history is practically universal in the modern world. Of course, there are some prophets of doom, especially in an age that fears nuclear or ecological destruction, and these prophets are able to make quite a case for their respective positions. But modern individuals have been basically optimistic. They live the greater portion of their present planning for and dreaming about a better future. Modern individuals have adapted to their peculiar environment; they have mastered the technique of pushing aside the uncertainties of life (at least on the surface of things) and tend to look upon themselves as immortal, indestructible, unique characters—sort of twentieth-century Nietzschean supermen. Needless to state, such an attitude carries with it a considerable degree of frustration, as most critics of the present age are quick to indicate. Nonetheless, this attitude on the part of modern individuals is widespread. It is the logical conclusion to the theory of indefinite progress, and perhaps only it can give people the crutch they need, having lost the security they had under the providence view.

An exceedingly influential progress view of history in the twentieth century has been the one formulated by Karl Marx during the 1800's. Popularly regarded only as the founder of modern communism, Marx is rarely thought of as a philosopher of history except in academic circles. Yet the *Communist Manifesto* is a philosophy of history. The basis of the Marxian system is found in the writings of the German idealistic philosopher, Hegel, and is known as the dialectic. The Hegelian dialectic was utilized by Marx, who claimed to have discovered an immutable and universal law of human history. Today the system of Karl Marx is commonly referred to as the Communist dialectic.

Human history, according to Marx, is the story of class struggle. Class relations are based on the mode of production of the individual—the role a person plays in the economic structure—and the productive role is the determining factor in history. People are primarily producing animals, and their economic status in relation to other individuals determines their social class. The existing dominant class always breeds its opposition because it is forcing the subservient class to put more of itself into what it is producing than what it receives for its effort. Therefore, there exists alienation, and the result is conflict, out of which a new class structure will develop. Marx even has an equation for this class struggle: Thesis plus antithesis equals synthesis. For example, the medieval aristocracy created its own opposition in the form of downtrodden serfs, but out of this structure the rising middle class, in turn, emerged. Everything is in a constant state of flux, and this is both good and inevitable. For according to the dialectic of Marxian communism, everything is as it should be at all times; even the allegedly oppressed workers in a capitalistic state are viewed as the manifestation of an "inevitable" stage toward a classless society.

As the various phases of this class struggle are realized and a new class structure is being created, progress is being achieved. The end of this bloody and drawn-out class struggle will be, according to Marx, the end of all struggle due to the abolition of all classes and the end of self-alienation; individuals will achieve complete freedom in a perfect communistic society. With this development, the Marxian equation eventually ceases to exist.

The adherent of the Marxian theory of progress is a secure person. An inevitable law has determined the eventual realization of the system, given the condition, of course, that the Marxian "law" is valid. The Marxian theory, which holds sway over a large portion of the modern-day world, is simply a typical progress view of history with a utopian climax on earth; it is one that has been adjusted, adapted, and put into practice by powerful political organizations.

Since the Marxian or communist dialectic assumes that society is in a constant state of flux, there concomitantly exists a constant changing and reinterpretation of "facts," i.e., frequent communist "revisions" of history. The communist dialectic generates and justifies historical revision as part of the dynamic process unfolding in history. Hence communist "facts" and the "facts" of the Western world are not necessarily the same. George Orwell's famous novel, *1984,* depicts this revisionist policy. What was becomes whatever the official party writings claim it to have been. Accurate knowledge according to Western standards is willingly sacrificed to faith in the inevitability of the dialectic process.

Another area where the progress theory is highly influential is within the United States. Admittedly, democracy rests on no concise, formalized philosophical system; and progress in America is based on no formalized philosophy of history. But progress is an integral part of modern American society—one need only to listen to the politicians talk about it during election years. What are the "Square Deals," "New Deals," "New Nationalisms," "New Freedoms," "New Frontiers," and "Great Societies" but various twentieth-century attempts by political leaders to implement a program of progress for the American people? What successful politician does not talk about moving ahead, improving life, etc., and what audience does not applaud such speeches?

4. Representative Philosophies of History

The cyclical view, the providential view, and the progress view comprise the three major historical interpretations that have been developed to date. History has also been subjected to various other interpretations, none of which, however, was or is as influential as those three. For the most part, other interpretations are adaptations and combinations of the three major theories. Still, they deserve at least brief mention, and the student of history would do well to be aware of them. What follows is a representative sampling of these viewpoints.[4]

People such as Condorcet (1743–1794) and Turgot (1727–1781) held that history is the recounting of a human progression from east to west. As new civilizations develop farther west, they are improved versions of older civilizations to the east. Progress is thereby achieved because people are improving; they are drawing upon the successes and failures of earlier societies in order to create a better one. This is a progress view, but it is a form of progress that is strongly determined by geography. It, too, is inevitable. The viewpoint is a curious mixture of what might be termed a limited geographical cyclicalism with progress as an end result. The cycle, incidentally, would supposedly end in the United States (both men were ardent admirers of American democracy); it would not keep circling the globe.

A minor offshoot of this geographical viewpoint is the climatic theory, of which the American, Ralph Waldo Emerson (1803–1882), was one notable exponent. This theory holds that superior civilizations can only develop in temperate zones. Those civiliza-

---

[4] As yet there is no basic survey work on philosophies of history suitable for a majority of lower division history students. Examples of advanced works are found in the bibliography.

tions existing elsewhere are extremely limited in the amount of progress they can achieve; those located in temperate zones may progress indefinitely. The reason is that temperature differences are held to provide a stimulus to greater activity, whereas people residing in consistently hot or cold environments become as stagnant as their surroundings.

G. W. F. Hegel (1770–1831), a philosophical idealist, believed history to be not only a bloody world struggle but also, at the same time, a rational process. History is in a fluid state; by the process of negation it moves in the direction of the absolute concrete universal—the *Geist*. Realization of the *Geist*, or absolute world spirit, will result from the submission of all individual spirits to the collective spirit; and the divine idea—the state—will be realized on earth. Realization of the *Geist* will bring an end to the negation process. At the same time, individuals will completely realize their freedom by submerging their individuality into the state, for the universal divine idea—the *Geist*—is only realized when it becomes universally accepted. This theory is a variant of the basic progress viewpoint.

Another thinker, August Comte (1798–1857), viewed history as a struggle in which change must inevitably take place. Human history consists of nothing more than one long struggle to discover the heretofore unknown, perfect laws of social living. These immutable laws exist, he claimed, but the human race will not necessarily discover them. Thus, the reputed father of modern sociology presented us with a potential earthly utopia as a possible end result. Comte was stating that there can be, but not necessarily will be, indefinite progress. Individuals possess the capacity for progress if they can but discover it.

Herbert Spencer (1820–1903) held that history is the movement from the homogeneous to the heterogeneous—from simple tribal systems to complex urban structures and from one-celled organisms to highly complex individuals. Cultures could decay and fall, just as individuals grow old and die, but the ultimate course of the human race is upward and onward. This is a form of inevitable progress, and its end is human perfection. Spencer was reflecting the extremely influential evolution theory as posited by Charles Darwin. Spencer's viewpoint remains quite popular to the present day and appears to be borne out by what is commonly regarded as twentieth-century progress.

Oswald Spengler (1880–1936) likened human cultures to the life cycles of human beings. All cultures are destined to follow identical patterns of progress and decay. History, according to Spengler, must be considered through the eyes of the biologist.

The view is cyclical, for historical time is simply the registration of the life process. Although the view is pessimistic, repudiating the progress view at a time when that view was flourishing, Spengler's work was widely read until Arnold Toynbee superseded it in 1927.

Toynbee (1889-   ) accepted part of Spengler's notions but was actually writing to repudiate them. He adopted Spengler's "cultures," which he termed "civilizations." These civilizations are people considered collectively, and they are subject to natural and biological laws. They all follow the same cycles. But unlike Spengler, Toynbee held that this does not necessarily continue. Civilization can progress, building upon past achievements as it goes along. The key is challenge and response. If a civilization is presented with a challenge to which it is able to respond adequately, growth occurs. And as a corollary to this, creative minorities stimulate the growth of the civilization of which they are a part. Much more optimistic than Spengler, Toynbee provides for progress in his view of history, blending the cyclical and progress views together.

We could go on and on. There are all sorts of other theories and interpretations (some are alluded to in Chapter 6). A number of these theories possess some degree of merit, whereas others are totally meaningless except to their formulators. But students must bear in mind the fact that regardless of their merit or lack of merit, all philosophies of history are only theories. They cannot be satisfactorily proven—even the meaningful ones. Most cannot be disproven either.

There is real merit in attempting to discover some sense and meaning in human history. Although some of these theories appear to be ridiculous, we should remain cognizant of the fact that they represent sincere attempts (even on the part of such a confused soul as Vico) to form some order out of the apparent chaos that is human history.

Individuals can learn to profit from their previous errors. So, too, can nations profit from their past mistakes. Perfectibility is to be sought, not as an end to be achieved necessarily, but as an ideal. This is the message of the great minds in human history.

Questions for Discussion

1.   What constitutes a philosophy of history? What are the advantages of possessing a philosophy of history?

2.   What is the significance of the cyclical view of history? The providential view?

3.   Account for the understanding of the past in light of the Soviet revisionist policy regarding history.

4.   What are the major characteristics of any progress view of history? What opportunities for individual flexibility exist in this view?

5.   In what ways is the progress view of the history of the philosophies of history reflected in this chapter? What would a narrative about philosophies of history look like if it were constructed from the cyclical view? The providential view?

6.   Evaluate some of the representative philosophies of history presented in this chapter in terms of your own understanding of the contemporary world. What insights (if any) do these philosophies of history give?

Historical Writing: Types and Techniques

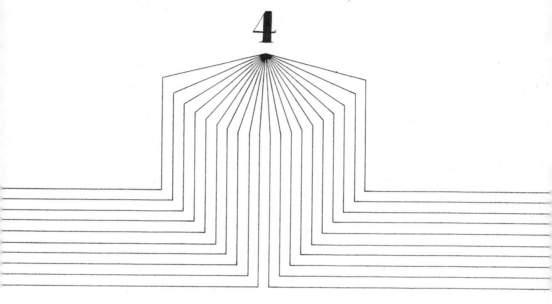

4

There are two broad categories of historical writing with which beginning students should be thoroughly familiar. One category consists of those materials upon which students must rely in order to acquire their historical fact. From the students' viewpoint, we may arbitrarily refer to these writings as "historical information materials." The other category is concerned with those types of writings that students will probably be required to submit as class assignments.

1. Historical Information Materials

Students of history should be familiar with, and possess a thorough working knowledge of, three basic types of historical writing that will provide them with their facts. These categories, each of which contains various forms, are: (A) primary works, both in published and in manuscript form; (B) secondary works, both published and unpublished; and (C) journal articles, which include magazine articles, newspaper accounts, and articles in the various professional historical journals.

A. PRIMARY WORKS Primary works are original source materials for historical fact—tangible materials which existed at the time the historical event was taking place and which aid in describing it. They include such items as eyewitness accounts, diaries, letters, and public documents (laws, treaties, hearings, court decisions, etc.). They may include photographs and newsreels, as well as artifacts discovered by archaeologists. Stamps, coins, coats of arms, seals, wills, genealogical tables, in fact, just about everything that can give us some clue to the past, if it is in its original, untampered form, may be classified as primary source material.

Written original sources do not have to be in their original manuscript form. But a primary work cannot be edited, other than in organization, and still be classified as a primary work. Published collections of Bismarck's personal correspondence, for instance, are primary materials, even though the compiler has probably arranged them in some sort of order, either by chronology or by subject. But an interpretation of Bismarck's correspondence, even though material is quoted extensively from it, is not a primary source; it has been altered. Similarly, a volume of American treaties is primary material but an interpretation of American foreign policy is not. Great care should be exercised in the use of newspaper accounts. They may be primary material, but they may also editorialize, thereby giving a slant to the past that might not be entirely accurate.

Historians utilize primary materials to acquire facts, which they then organize, interpret, and formulate into the reconstruction of a bygone event. They must always provide the interpretation when they are working with primary source materials.

It is unlikely that beginning students of history will make much use of primary materials except, perhaps, for some of the excellent published collections now available, which might be incorporated into a term paper. They might also make use of family records or letters, and these are classified as primary materials. But the use of primary materials (even in published form) usually falls within the domain of graduate students and professional historians; and unpublished primary materials are even more their fare.

B. SECONDARY WORKS The bulk of materials used by beginning history students will be secondary source materials. As the term implies, secondary materials are one step removed from primary materials. Secondary works are the end products of the study and use of primary materials by historians, to which they have added their own organization and interpretation. This does not mean that historians acquire all of their facts for secondary works from primary sources alone. They may rely heavily on

primary materials, but they also consult many other secondary
works and journal articles. They legitimately take full advantage
of the research of fellow historians—and the historical fraternity
encourages them in this practice. Then historians synthesize the
material obtained from all sources, provide their own interpretive
structure based on the facts, and thereby produce secondary
works. By testing the interpretations of earlier historians against
the latest historical evidence, contemporary historians are better
able to approach historical accuracy.

All textbooks and monographs are secondary works. So are
collections of primary materials if they have been substantively
edited or interpreted by their author. In fact, any primary material
that has been altered in content becomes a secondary work. It is
with these secondary works that beginning history students will
develop their greatest acquaintance and use.

C. JOURNAL ARTICLES   Beginning history students will also
make some use of journal articles. Although much shorter in
length than books, journal articles are secondary materials offering
much practical information. Articles in professional historical journals yield a great deal of oftentimes not readily accessible fact.[1]
The pedantic style characteristic of many journal articles, however,
often seems to be quite dull and boring to the novice historian
(once a real interest in history is developed, however, this attitude
will disappear). Although articles in popular magazines and newspapers offer the advantages of popularly written language and
interesting formats, a very serious disadvantage is the fact that
both the information and the interpretations contained in them
may be unreliable.[2]

2. Types of Student Historical Writing

The above are the types of historical writings that students will
rely on for basic fact and information. But they do not constitute
the types of writing that they will be called upon to produce as
class assignments. Five basic forms of historical writing may be
required of beginning students: book reports, journal article reports, book reviews, journal article reviews, and term papers.

Students should be thoroughly familiar with the differences
among these various writing forms. As far as their exact styling is
concerned, some colleges and universities have published their own

---

[1] The bibliography contains a representative list of some of the major historical
journals.

[2] The problem of reliability of newspaper articles is handled very well in Allan
Nevins, *Gateway to History* (rev. ed.; Boston: D. C. Heath and Company, 1962).

style sheets. If a given institution does not have an established style, individual instructors may possibly develop their own format. Because of these possibilities, what follows is simply a description of the content and approaches of these various writing forms. However, in the absence of special instructions to the contrary, the student would be safe in following the suggestions and guidelines indicated below.

A. BOOK REPORTS   Book reports are a customary type of assignment for lower division history students. A book report is a summary of the contents, plot, or thesis of a particular book preceded by a full bibliographical citation. The writer of a book report is not required to evaluate the author's work, although the writer often does so. Book reports vary in length, depending on the individual preferences of the instructor. Usually, however, a book report is limited to two or three double-spaced typewritten pages. Book reports indicate whether students have read the book and whether or not they understand sufficiently what they have read. It is one of the easiest assignments students will receive.

B. JOURNAL ARTICLE REPORTS   A journal article report is very similar to a book report in that it is primarily a summary of an article. It does not usually contain an evaluation. Journal article reports are often a favored assignment of the history instructor because the student is capable of writing quite a number of them in the same length of time required to handle one book report. Consequently, the student is given a greater breadth of historical materials, receives a wider acquaintanceship with writers of history, and becomes familiar with the various historical journals.

C. BOOK REVIEWS   A book review is a critical analysis of a book, preceded by a full bibliographical citation of the work being reviewed.[3] It does not summarize the contents of the book. Rather, it is an evaluation of the author's technique, organization, and thesis. In professional reviews widely known fact within the book receives little or no attention, and the reviewer concentrates on evaluating what is new or different in it. The professional book reviewer requires a fairly thorough knowledge both of the subject area with which the book deals and of all related literature. For this reason the book review is usually quite difficult for the beginning student. It is sometimes preferred by the instructor, however, because it demonstrates knowledge and understanding in a very short paper and requires a considerable amount of thought and planning.

[3] Consult the bibliographical citations contained in Appendix A for examples of style and sequence.

D. JOURNAL ARTICLE REVIEWS A journal article review, paralleling the book review, is a critical analysis of the work under consideration. The only real difference is that the work being reviewed is an article in a periodical rather than a full-length book. Otherwise the procedure and contents are the same. However, a journal article review is usually limited to one page or less. A decided advantage of the journal article review is that a number of such reviews can be assigned without overburdening the student, and this consequently introduces the student to a broader range of materials and authors.

E. THE TERM PAPER[4] By far the most difficult writing assignment (and research assignment as well) that students will encounter is the term paper. In order to write a term paper in history they must read a number of secondary works and journal articles on a particular topic, and then integrate the information acquired from these sources into their own ordering and interpretation of the topic.

The thesis that is presented, i.e., the interpretive structure being given to the facts, need not be that of the student. Students are perfectly free to use the ideas and points of view found in the works that they have read. But they must, under all circumstances, cite the sources of their information and ideas, giving full credit whenever it is due. Students should never quote from works or make use of the ideas of other writers without informing their reader. Otherwise, they would be guilty of the extremely serious offense of plagiarism—a form of cheating.

In order to maintain complete intellectual honesty in the use of material, the term paper should be footnoted. And because footnoting is both very important and very complex the next section is devoted to it. The term paper should also contain a bibliography, i.e., a properly cited list of all the materials that were utilized in the writing of the paper.

The length of the term paper will vary, depending on the individual preferences of the instructor. If no guidelines are prescribed, ten to fifteen typewritten pages, double spaced, would usually constitute an adequate length for the body of the paper. It should be preceded by a title page and a table of contents and completed with a bibliography.

The term paper is an excellent exercise in historical method, for not only must students seek out and evaluate their materials, thereby gaining good library experience and basic research tech-

---

[4] For a very detailed consideration on the nature of historical writing, see Sherman Kent, *Writing History* (2nd ed.; New York: Appleton-Century-Crofts, Inc., 1967), available in paperback.

nique, but also they are forced to integrate material in a logical fashion and supply continuity to their presentation. Coupled with this, the term paper provides an excellent exercise in the mechanics of historical writing, i.e., the use of footnotes and bibliography mentioned above. And finally, the term paper provides good training in historical reading—historians are rapid, voluminous readers, and the ability to read rapidly with comprehension comes only through practice.

CHOOSING A TOPIC   Great care should be exercised in selecting a topic for a term paper. First of all, students should decide upon a topic that, if at all possible, is of considerable interest to themselves. They will be working with it for some time, and if they do not find it personally interesting, a potentially satisfying task will turn into an unpleasant chore. Second, students must ascertain whether or not adequate materials are available on the subject in which they are interested. They should begin by going to the various reference works listed in the bibliography at the end of this book. These reference works will guide them to the necessary literature for their topic. Third, they should check their reference list against the library card catalog in order to determine the availability of a sufficient number of pertinent works to provide them with enough information to write a paper. Many a student has spent dozens of hours working on a particular topic and then discovered that sufficient materials were unavailable. Proper preliminary research can prevent this from happening.

In checking the library for materials students should always carefully fill out a bibliography card for each pertinent work that they locate. This procedure has a twofold purpose. It will eventually prove a time-saver by keeping them from having to recheck the library if they decide to use a particular work in writing their papers. And it will provide the necessary information for a full bibliographic entry at the end of the paper or for a footnote citation in the text.

For the bibliography card, a standard 3 × 5-in. index card is recommended, but any uniform card or sheet is satisfactory provided only that it is not so large as to prove unwieldy and that it is durable (the card will be handled a great deal). The student should be very careful to avoid placing more than one bibliographical citation on each card; otherwise, organizational difficulties may be encountered later.

At the lower left (there is no set rule, just tradition) students should place the library call number. This is to be done strictly for their own convenience so that they will not have to recheck the library card catalog at a later date for the same work. And it should be pointed out that some professors may require the catalog number as part of the bibliographical entry.

The bibliography card takes the following form:

Kurtz, Stephen G. *The Presidency of John Adams.* Philadelphia: The University of Pennsylvania Press, 1957.

Cat. #

Note that the last name of the author appears first (as in the library card catalog), followed by the first name and middle initial, followed by a period. The complete title of the work comes next, again followed by a period. Underlining (italicizing) the title on the bibliography card is optional. After the title are placed all of the pertinent facts of publication, such as the number of volumes, edition of the work, revision, editor, or translator. Then comes the location of publication, followed by a colon, the name of the publisher, followed by a comma, and finally, the copyright date or date of publication, followed by a period.

The form used in filling out a bibliography card as explained and illustrated above is the same for a bibliographical citation with two minor exceptions: one, the library catalog number is usually not included in the bibliographical citation, and two, the title of any work should always be underlined (the form used to indicate italics) wherever it appears in the paper, whereas it is not necessary to underline it on a bibliography card. But possible error can be avoided by getting into the habit of underlining all titles, whether necessary or not, as was done in the illustration (indicated by italics).

Also, in the bibliographical entry it is often the practice to annotate the entry, i.e., to indicate in a few short phrases or a sentence the particular usefulness of that work. An annotated bibliography is usually far more meaningful and informative to the reader than a straight bibliographical entry. Examples of this technique are to be found in Appendix A at the end of this work. One suggestion: if the student plans to annotate his or her bibliography (and the instructor might make this a requirement), it would be a good idea to jot down appropriate comments on the back of the bibliography card immediately after reading the work, lest, by the time the bibliography is being written, perhaps two months later, part of the impression and utility of the work might be forgotten.

NOTE TAKING   Having selected a topic and having determined the availability of materials, the writer of the term paper is now ready to begin gathering information by reading the selected works and taking notes on them. The taking of proper notes is extremely important. It can result in the saving of tremendous amounts of time, and it can lessen the possibility of factual error in the term paper.

Students quite often experience considerable difficulty in taking notes properly. Either they take far too many notes or far too few. It would be better to take too many notes than too few, but such a procedure is a waste of time and effort. It would definitely be better to use the time and effort to learn the techniques of proper note-taking.

Students at the lower division level who take too many notes either are afraid that they might be missing something, or, and this is more often the reason, are not really certain about what they are going to write. Consequently they are not really sure what to look for in their reading. This is oftentimes the result of not having selected a topic carefully. There is no single answer to this difficulty, but simple guidelines can be suggested.

Always remember that notes are to be taken only on what is really important or complex and only if they aid in understanding a particular viewpoint. Paragraphs or pages should normally not be copied from a secondary work verbatim. Experienced notetakers summarize the material *in their own words,* for this is an excellent personal test of their understanding of what they have just read. Notes pertaining to different ideas and topics, or coming from different works, should always be written on separate sheets usually a 5 × 7-in. size, including the page number or numbers on which the material was located. Thus, if the note is actually used in writing the term paper the writer will have all necessary information for a footnote citation in his or her possession. Above all else, the student should always avoid taking notes continuously on sheets of paper as if he or she were taking down notes in a lecture or studying from the course textbook. Notes written in this continuous manner are of practically no use in organizing and writing a term paper.

Cardinal rule number one: Notes should always be taken in the notetaker's own words, with no more than one idea or topic on a single note card.

It cannot be emphasized enough that the student should avoid taking notes in the exact words of the author whom he or she is reading, unless a particular statement lends considerable support to the term paper thesis or is extremely succinct. And when quoting verbatim, quotation marks should always be used. The term paper should not consist of page upon page of long, direct quotations from some text, occasionally linked together by a sentence or two written by the student (though some papers, by the very nature of the topic, will require considerably more direct quotation than other papers). The history instructor is interested in determining whether or not the student has successfully integrated and developed materials taken from a variety of sources.

On the other hand, it is not prudent to be parsimonious in taking notes. If the student should happen to come upon a strong idea, one which concisely supports a portion of his or her paper, it would be a good idea to copy pertinent portions of it verbatim on a note card, particularly if there is a distinct possibility that he or she will quote the material directly in the term paper. This procedure will avoid the possible necessity of being required to recheck the work later. But the student should not get upset by the fact that in the actual writing of the paper he may not make use of every tiny note taken during his reading. Students have a tendency of forcing material into a paper whether it belongs there or not, just because they have the material on a note card. Only a fraction of notes taken will actually be used in the paper.

Always remember that when one copies material verbatim, it may need editing. Sentences or phrases that are not pertinent should be deleted. This is done by inserting three successive dots between quoted materials. The dots indicate to the reader that something has been omitted. If an entire paragraph is omitted, this should be indicated by a line of asterisks. If the writer adds words to quoted material in order to bridge or explain omitted sections, they should be enclosed in brackets. And to avoid confusion, always place quotation marks around material that is taken down verbatim.

The student should be very careful to indicate exact pagination of quoted materials on his or her note cards, especially if the materials span more than a single page. Indicate on the note card exactly where the page change occurs. Again, this might save time later on, for in the actual writing of the paper, the student may discover that he or she only wants to quote a portion of the material and will know thereby exactly where it appeared.

Cardinal rule number two: Students should copy pertinent material verbatim only when they feel that there is a strong probability that they will use the material verbatim in their term papers, although they should not feel obligated to do so.

By way of a final observation, as stated before, if students are going to take notes properly, they must have a clear idea what they are going to write. This reflects the thoroughness of their initial research and thought in choosing a topic.

Cardinal rule number three: Students should know exactly what they are looking for before they begin detailed reading. When they find what they are looking for, then, and only then, should they take notes on it.

Once reading has been completed, the student should then categorize all note cards from all sources according to date, topic, person, or some other mode of classification that corresponds to the proposed organization of the term paper. If a chronological organization is intended, categorize notes according to date. If a topical approach is anticipated, categorize by event. No matter what approach is utilized, the student will thus accumulate stacks of note cards which will apply to a given chapter or other unit within the term paper. This is one very good method of integrating the various materials consulted in researching the term paper topic.

Experienced students develop more sophisticated techniques for categorizing notes. Some use different colored cards for different categories. Others use key punch cards, punching out a certain slot for a certain topic. All cards are then placed in a box with a coded card in the front indicating which slot represents which topic. A knitting needle, or some similar device, is inserted through the stack and raised. All cards pertaining to a given topic will then fall out of the stack. Various commercial devices based on this technique are now available. The student who plans a career in history might do well to check into these laborsaving devices.

When the instructor begins reading a term paper and discovers that only one work is cited repeatedly for the first half-dozen pages, then a different work only is cited for the next half-dozen pages, and so forth, he immediately suspects, with considerable justification, that the student has not taken good notes and has not organized his or her notes properly. It is evident that the student has not successfully integrated his or her materials—one of the most important goals of a term paper assignment. Only by correct note-taking procedure is the student able to properly organize and integrate various materials. One final note: Never underestimate your instructors. They are trained historians, and it is fairly easy for them to determine whether or not you have proceeded properly in a term paper assignment.

From what has been said, it would seem that writing a term paper is a rather difficult task. It is, but if students proceed with a positive attitude and have chosen a topic in which they are really interested, it can be a rather pleasant and rewarding task. A great deal of satisfaction can be derived from constructing such a paper.

It is hoped that these suggestions on note-taking will guide the student in organizing and writing a better term paper. But what has already been stated is not quite enough information for writing a good term paper in a history class. The student must also be able to document material accurately and according to accepted procedures. The student must know the mechanics of good historical writing.

Proper footnoting technique is probably one of the most difficult procedures for the student to master. Fortunately there exists a fairly well-accepted set of rules that govern footnote citation.

3. Types and Use of Footnotes

Footnotes may be of two types: reference and content. Reference footnotes are used either to cite an authority for statements, quotations, or ideas presented in the text, or to refer to materials and authorities cited previously. Content footnotes provide elaboration on material found in the body of the text which is somewhat tangential and might destroy continuity but at the same time is interesting and relevant. A content footnote may also be employed to acknowledge some individual or work that is not actually being used in the work, but which contains useful information on the same subject.[5]

Footnoting should be performed both systematically and discriminately. First of all, let us consider the system employed. Footnotes should be assigned arabic numbers in ascending order, i.e., 1, 2, 3, 4, 5, etc., beginning anew on each page, beginning anew with each chapter (the method employed in this book), or running continuously throughout the entire work. No number should ever be skipped or repeated. If a footnote is added or deleted during the course of writing a paper, all subsequent footnotes must be renumbered accordingly. This is one good reason for using the chapter numbering technique rather than numbering through the entire work—it saves a great deal of effort if a footnote is added or subtracted.

In the body of the text the arabic number should immediately follow the material being footnoted, and it should be placed approximately one-half line above the line of the textual material in the very next space following punctuation marks, if any (the only

---

[5] All of the preceding footnotes contained in this work would fit into this category. They simply refer the reader to particularly good works for further reading and elaboration. This note, incidentally, is strictly a content footnote.

exception is if the punctuation mark is a dash). Note the following illustrations.

". . . and as a result the war came to an end."[3]
"I have but one life to give for my country."[4]
There is no real basis for this idea,[5] but we should . . .

Bear in mind that the arabic number is to be placed at the end of the material being quoted or acknowledged if it is a reference footnote (the first two examples above). It may possibly be placed near the beginning or even in the middle of a sentence if it is a content footnote (third example above). As is the case with the reference footnote, the content footnote should be placed as closely as possible to the material to which it refers, provided only that it does not destroy the continuity of the sentence. Good discretionary judgment should prevail.

Every footnote number found in the text of a page must also have its counterpart at the foot of the same page (an exceptionally long footnote may begin on one page and carry over to the foot of the next page, but this rarely happens). Proper spacing must be allowed for footnotes in the typing of the paper. At the bottom of the page the same footnote number that is found in the body of the text is to be placed immediately preceding the footnote material, and it is to be raised approximately one-half line above it, with no spacing between the number and the footnote material. The first line of a footnote should be indented in the same manner as a paragraph in the text. Subsequent lines should be single spaced, whereas all material in the body of the text should be double spaced. In published works the footnote type is smaller than the type used in the text. The above procedure is simply the typist's way of indicating the same delineation. Note the following examples of footnote citation, paying especial heed to spacing.

[13] Patrick Gardiner, *Theories of History* (Glencoe, Illinois: The Free Press, 1959), p.—.
[14] John Bury, *The Idea of Progress* (London: Macmillan and Company, Ltd., 1921), p.—.

A reference footnote must contain the following information in the exact order as it is listed (refer to the preceding examples): full name of the author, complete title of the work, all facts of publication, and the exact location in the work from which the material is being extracted. Let us now consider each of these units of footnote information in detail, indicating proper punctuation.

A. NAME   The complete name of the author in its normal form is indicated first. It is followed by a comma. No titles such as Mr., Dr., or Professor are used. It should be pointed out that an author may be an institution, committee, or agency as well as an individual; the same format prevails. Examples of authors other than individuals are: United States, Office of Education; United States Senate, Committee on the Judiciary; American Federation of Labor; and Metropolitan Church Federation.

Some works have more than one author. If there are three authors or less, list every one of them according to the procedure already outlined. If there are more than three authors, list only the name of the first author appearing on the title page of the work, followed by the underlined (italicized) words *"et al.,"* the Latin abbreviation which means "and others." If the work is a compilation or anthology, list only the name of the principal editor, followed by the abbreviation (ed.) in parentheses as indicated, followed by a comma (if the principal editor is unknown, list the names of all the editors). Note the following examples of author citation.

Karl Lowith. [One author only]
United States Senate, Committee on the Judiciary. [Author is an agency or institution]
Oscar T. Barck and Nelson M. Blake. [Three or fewer authors]
Wood Gray, *et al.* [More than three authors]
Robert Maynard Hutchins (ed.). [An editor of a work]

Occasionally works that do not have a known author may be consulted. Three procedures may be employed under these circumstances. One is simply to begin the footnote citation with the exact title, followed by the facts of publication, and so on. When this procedure is used it is assumed that the reader will understand that there is no known author. The assumption is not quite valid, because there are some works that have no author (refer to the citations in the bibliography for examples of this). Hence, the reader does not know if there is no author or no known author—this constitutes quite a difference. Another technique is to use the term *"non auctoris"* in lieu of the author's name. Although the term literally means "no author," it is widely understood to mean that there is an author for the work but that his name is not known. A third technique is to use the abbreviation "Anon.," for anonymous.

B. TITLE   The title of the book or other type of publication is cited next exactly as it appears on the title page. Even if the

spelling, capitalization, or punctuation are incorrect in the title, it
should be listed exactly as it appears. The insertion of the abbreviation *"sic."* in brackets indicates to the reader that the error is not
that of the writer of the paper but the error of the author or publisher, or both. The only exception to the rule indicated occurs
when the work in question carries a subtitle. In this instance the
main title is to be listed, followed by the subtitle, but with a colon
inserted between the two titles (added punctuation); in some cases
a colon appears on the title page and, hence, its addition would be
unnecessary. The entire title should always be underlined (i.e., it
should be italicized, and this is indicated by underlining it).

If the title is that of an article within a periodical, the title of
the article should be placed within quotation marks, followed by
the title of the periodical itself. Only the periodical title should be
underlined. The article title and the periodical title should be sepa-
rated by a comma. Study the following illustrations carefully.

[1] Karl Lowith, *Meaning in History.* [An example of an exact
title of a book]
[2] Oscar T. Barck and Nelson M. Blake, *Since 1900: A History
of the United States in Our Times.* [A book with a subtitle and
added punctuation (the colon)]
[3] Julius W. Pratt, "The Origins of Manifest Destiny," *American
Historical Review.* [An article within a periodical with proper
punctuation]

The first line of a footnote, it should be recalled, must be indented
in the same manner as a paragraph. The second and succeeding
lines of a footnote begin at the margin and are single spaced. Again,
note the illustrations above.

Following the title there may be a reference to the compiler or
editor of the work. This can be a little confusing, especially since
an editor's name can also precede the work. But certain rules govern its placement. If one author is writing about the works of another author and quoting his material extensively, or if he is collecting various materials from numerous authors, as in an anthology, his name precedes the work followed by (ed.), as already
indicated. However, if he is composing a new edition of an already
existing work by a different author, the other author's name comes
first, followed by the title of the work, followed by the name of
the editor preceded by the abbreviation "ed.," which is *not* placed
in parenthesis.

C. **FACTS OF PUBLICATION**   All the facts of publication pertaining to a work are set off by parentheses in the footnote (but

not in the bibliography). The opening of the parentheses comes either immediately after the title with no intervening punctuation, or after the name of the editor, if an editor's name follows the title, with no intervening punctuation.

The facts of publication include, first of all, the number of volumes in the work, if the work consists of more than a single volume. If no indication of volumes is given in the reference, the reader may safely assume that the work is a single volume. The number of volumes is always indicated by an arabic number, followed by the abbreviation "vols." Examples are: 4 vols., 13 vols., etc. Never capitalize the abbreviated version of "volumes" in a footnote citation pertaining to the facts of publication.

After the number of volumes, if any, comes the edition number of the work. If no edition is indicated, the reader may safely assume that the work is a first edition. The edition of the work is expressed according to the following illustrations: rev. ed., 2nd ed., 4th ed., and 6th ed. This information is shown on the title page of the work. Do not confuse it with the number of printings, which may also be indicated. A suggestion that will avoid confusion is to refer to the latest edition and copyright date indicated. Each edition has to be copyrighted separately, because technically it is a different work. Although all copyright dates may be indicated in the work, always use only the most recent one.

It will quite often happen that neither one of these first two facts of publication will be applicable to a work. But the other facts of publication will always be applicable. If only one of these first two facts is cited, it is to be followed with a semicolon. If both should happen to be applicable, separate them with a comma and follow the second fact with a semicolon.

The next fact of publication is concerned with the place where the work was published. Note that this refers to the location of publication, not of writing. Simply indicate the city where it was published. This information may be obtained from the title page of the work. If the title page makes mention of several cities, cite only the name of the first. If the city listed is not one that would be immediately known to most readers, include either the state or the nation, whichever is more appropriate, after a comma. The place of publication is followed by a colon.

The complete name of the publishing company, as found on the title page, follows the colon. Many historians do not list the publishing company in their citations, and some history departments omit it by established policy. If the student chooses to omit the citation in the footnote, he should place it in the bibliography. Follow the preferences of the instructor making the assignment.

After the name of the publishing company, if it is being indicated, place a comma followed by the copyright date alluded to above. If no copyright date is indicated in the work, this fact can be made known to the reader by the symbol "n. d.," which stands for "no date indicated." If the copyright date is determined from some source other than the work itself, it should be indicated, but place it in brackets. If the work was written over a period of years, indicate such information according to the following procedure: 1952-1957, 1817-1842, or 1968-1969. And if it is a multi-volumed work that is still in the process of being written and published, give the date when publication began, followed by a dash: the dash indicates that the total work is not yet completed and that other volumes are to appear at a later date. Relevant examples of this form are to be found in the bibliography.

The date concludes the facts of publication. This should be indicated by closing the parentheses and adding a period. For example:

[15] Donald Sheehan, *The Making of American History* (2 vols., rev. ed.; New York: The Dryden Press, 1954).

D. LOCATION OF REFERENCED MATERIAL   The last portion of the reference footnote citation concerns the exact portion of the work from which the material footnoted is being drawn or quoted. If the work is a multi-volumed work, first list the volume number. This is designated by a roman numeral, e.g., I, II, III, IV. No mention of the word "volume" is necessary; this has been taken care of in the facts of publication. Also, note that the number of volumes in the facts of publication is designated by an arabic number. The reason for this switch in number forms will become evident in a moment.

Follow the volume number with a comma and add the page number. If one page is being referred to, write "p. 17." If several continuous pages are being referred to, write "pp. 17-22." If two or more different pages, which are not continuous, are being referred to, write "pp. 45 and 51." This, however, is only done when the same idea is being expressed in various parts of the work. Separate ideas and separate quotations must be cited separately.

Now we can explain the reason for the roman numeral being used to express the volume number in the citation; it is that "IV, p. 4" is much less confusing for the reader than "4, p. 4."

There is only one exception to the volume number procedure as outlined above. This has to do with reference to articles that appear in periodicals. Instead of the volume number appearing

after the facts of publication, it comes immediately after the title
of the periodical. The reason for this is that there are no such facts
of publication applying to periodicals as there are to books. The
volume number of a periodical follows the periodical title, preceded by a comma, as follows: "XXVI." It is followed by the year
and the month of publication (certain periodicals such as newspapers might require the exact date and these are enclosed by
parentheses and followed by a comma. Last comes the citing of
the page number. This requires no elaborate comment; it is identical in form to that of the book citation. The edition, location
and name of the publisher, and the number of volumes of the periodical as a fact of publication do not apply to periodical citations.
Note the difference between a book citation and a periodical citation in the following illustration.

[1] Thomas A. Bailey, *A Diplomatic History of the American
People* (4th ed.; New York: Appleton-Century-Crofts, Inc., 1950),
p.—.
    [2] G. B. Adams, "History and the Philosophy of History,"
American Historical Review, XIV (1909), p. 769.

Mention should also be made of the proper form for citing
those government documents that are frequently utilized by historians. The most frequently used documents are court decisions,
the citing of laws, and proceedings contained in the official congressional publications.

A Supreme Court case is cited according to the following sequence: name of the case, information on where the case can be
located, and date of the decision. For example, *Hepburn* v.
Griswold, 8 Wallace 603 (February 7, 1870), is a complete Supreme Court citation. The names of legal cases (plaintiff and
defendant) should be underlined (italicized) and followed by a
comma. The location of the case information is a bit more complex and will be taken up momentarily. It is followed by the date
on which the Court actually rendered its decision. This date should
be enclosed in parentheses, and normally the year of the decision
is sufficient. Occasionally, however, it might be necessary to cite
the month and day of the decision.

With regard to the location of case information, "8 Wallace
603" means that the decision may be found in volume 8, page
603, of the Court Reports during the period when a man named
Wallace was the Clerk of the Court. Thus, many different names
will appear, e.g., Peters, Howard, and Wheaton, until late in 1875
when a new procedure was adopted. From that time on, the name

of the clerk was dropped, and in its place is used the simple term "U. S.," which stands for United States Supreme Court Reports. An example of this would be: *Tot* v. *United States,* 319 U. S. 463 (June 7, 1943).

The citing of decisions from other types of courts is handled in about the same manner. Only the location of the case information will vary. And since there are so many variations of this (literally hundreds), the student should consult specialized guides in political science for guidelines, should the need arise.

The procedure for citing federal laws is quite simple. Such material is cited according to the following form: 46 *Stat.* 21 (1929). This signifies that the law will be found in volume 46 of the *United States Statutes,* beginning on page 21, and was passed in 1929. Other legislative bodies follow a similar pattern. However, the variances are so many that what holds for the citing of non-Supreme Court cases also holds true here.

Materials recording congressional proceedings that are not laws follow the same general form used to cite a federal law. There are only two exceptions to this: (1) *United States Statutes* is replaced by an abbreviated form of *Congressional Record, Congressional Globe,* etc., and (2) any additional information that will more accurately direct the reader to the source should be included. Note the following two illustrations.

[4] 88 *Congressional Record* 7044, 77th Cong., 2nd sess. (September 7, 1942).

[5] 81 *Congressional Record,* Part V, 5639, Senate Report No. 711 (June 14, 1937).

For the minute details of citation, and for unusual or rarely used citation material, the reader is referred to one of the several excellent advanced guides available.[6]

For the benefit of the reader, sample footnotes are presented below. While reading them pay special attention to the placement of punctuation marks and the sequence of citation material. All of the materials listed constitute excellent sources for further study in history (depending on personal interests, of course), and they are highly recommended. Page and volume numbers are included for illustration purposes only, except for journal articles and government documents. They do not refer to any particular item on the page, nor has any material been quoted from these works.

[6] One of the best works is: Kate L. Turabian, *A Manual for Writers of Term Papers, Theses, and Dissertations* (rev. ed.; Chicago: The University of Chicago Press, 1955).

Footnotes may be cited at the foot of each page as they occur, or they may be collected at the end of each chapter, or at the end of the entire work. Follow the preference of your instructor.

¹ Arnold Toynbee, *A Study of History* (12 vols.; New York: Oxford University Press, 1934-1961), VIII, p. 831.

² Elmer Ellis, "The Profession of Historian," *Mississippi Valley Historical Review*, XXXVIII (1951), pp. 3-20. [Illustrations of periodical citations list correct volume numbers. The pages refer to the exact pages within the periodical concerning the article.]

³ Michael Kraus, *The Writing of American History* (Norman: The University of Oklahoma Press, 1953), p. 350.

⁴ *Corporation of Brick Church* v. *Mayor, et al.*, 5 Cowen (N. Y.) 538 (1826). [This is an example of a state court decision citation.]

⁵ A. L. Rowse, *The Expansion of Elizabethan England* (London: Macmillan and Company, Ltd., 1955), p. 700.

⁶ Worthington C. Ford and Gaillard Hunt (eds.), *The Journals of the Continental Congress* (34 vols.; Washington: Government Printing Office, 1904-07), XIII, p. 67.

⁷ Hiram M. Chittenden, *The American Fur Trade of the Far West* (2 vols.; New York: The Press of the Pioneers, Inc., 1935), I, p. 789.

⁸ Francis Parkman, *France and England in North America*, ed. Samuel E. Morison (London: Faber and Faber, 1956), p. 999.

⁹ F. Lee Benns, *Europe Since 1914: In Its World Setting* (8th ed.; New York: Appleton-Century-Crofts, Inc., 1954), p. 53.

¹⁰ 37 *Stat.* 699 (1913). [This is a federal law citation.]

¹¹ Board of Governors of the Federal Reserve System, *The Federal Reserve System: Purposes and Functions* (5th ed.; Washington: Division of Administrative Services, Board of Governors of the Federal Reserve System, 1964), p. 78.

¹² Ross M. Robertson, *History of the American Economy* (2nd ed.; New York: Harcourt, Brace & World, 1964), p. 566.

¹³ *Muskrat* v. *United States*, 219 U. S. 346 (1911).

¹⁴ Meribeth Cameron, Thomas Mahoney, and George McReynolds, *China, Japan and the Powers* (2nd ed; New York: The Ronald Press, 1960), p. 555.

¹⁵ U.S., *Congressional Record*, Vol. LXXXI, Part V, Senate Report No. 777, p. 5639. [The reader is cautioned of the fact that government document references fit no exact pattern. Record all pertinent information starting from the most general and working toward the particular.]

¹⁶ Herman Ausubel, *et al.* (eds.), *Some Modern Historians of Britain* (New York: The Dryden Press, 1951), p. 600.

[17] *Ware* v. *Hylton,* 3 Dallas 199 (1797).

[18] New York *Evening Post,* March 15, 1862, p. 7. [For newspaper citations simply list the name of the paper with the city of publication if not in the name, the date, and the volume if available. Underline the official title of the paper.]

[19] William T. Hutchinson, "The American Historian in Wartime," *Mississippi Valley Historical Review,* XXIX (September, 1942), pp. 163–186. [The date is important when the issues in a volume are paginated separately. If the entire volume is paginated consecutively, it is not necessary to include either the issue number or the date.]

[20] Elliot Roosevelt (ed.), *FDR: His Personal Letters 1928–1945* (2 vols.; New York: Duell, Sloan and Pearce, 1950), II, p. 900.

E. **THE CONTENT FOOTNOTE**   The content footnote possesses no set style. It is numbered in exactly the same manner as is the reference footnote. All footnotes are numbered continuously whether they are reference or content or, as is usually the case, a combination of the two. Spacing and indentation are identical. The only difference is that instead of a citation, the content footnote contains subject matter, usually to the extent of a very short paragraph but occasionally consisting of only a brief sentence. A few samples of content footnotes appear on the illustration pages that follow at the end of this chapter.

There is one variation of the use of the content footnote. This is used to refer the reader to another section or page within the work. It is technically known as the cross-reference footnote. Most frequently the cross-reference footnote is written as follows: [4] *Supra,* p. 67., or [4] *Infra,* p. 67., meaning that the reader is referred to p. 67 of the work for a further elaboration or review of similar type material. *Supra* translates as "above," and *Infra* translates as "below." Some writers prefer to use the terms "above" and "below" (being recommended by more and more style books) instead of their Latin forms, or even to write a sentence in the footnote explaining the cross reference. All of these forms are acceptable, but once the writer has used one of them, he should not use any other form within that particular work. The various forms should not be intermingled.

Caution and sound thought should always be employed in footnoting. Unfortunately, some students suffer from an uncontrollable tendency to overload their papers with footnotes, believing that the papers will consequently appear more scholarly. However, a heavily footnoted paper does not necessarily reflect solid scholarship. A rule that should always be followed is this:

Never footnote unless necessary for acknowledgement or clarity. The ability to footnote, in itself, does not necessarily make either a good historian or a good student of history. Good judgment in footnoting is far more important.

The procedure outlined above concerning the styling of reference footnotes applies only to initial references to a particular work. Later references to previously cited works may be shortened in a variety of ways. The student should always bear in mind, however, that he must remain with whatever method of shortening he initially chooses to follow; the various methods are not interchangeable within a given work. And it should be pointed out that it is not necessary to shorten later references to previously cited works. The initial procedure may very properly be repeated throughout the paper. However, when there is a simpler and shorter way of doing something, why not use it?

The simplest, and a perfectly acceptable, method is to cite later reference to a work in an abbreviated fashion. When this method is used the exact mode of abbreviation should be indicated in the first full reference to the work, lest the reader be confused. The following first reference footnote gives an illustration as to how this should be done.

[18] Gilbert J. Garraghan, *A Guide to Historical Method*, ed. Jean Delanglez (New York: Fordham University Press, 1946), p.—. Hereafter cited as Garraghan, *Guide*.

This indicates to the reader that all future references to the work will be cited only as Garraghan, *Guide*, plus the appropriate page number. It should be borne in mind that when this method is employed, no other method may be used. The principal advantages are that it is very simple to use and very easy to follow.

A more scholarly technique is to use the Latin abbreviations *ibid.*, *op. cit.*, and *loc. cit.* when referring to the works that have been previously cited in full form. This, of course, presupposes the fact that these abbreviations are understood and are used in the correct manner.

The term *"ibid."* is the abbreviation for *ibidem*, meaning "in the same place." It is used under only two conditions.

1. In a reference to an article within a periodical, the term *ibid.* may be used to refer to the title of the periodical if another article from the same periodical is quoted in the very next footnote. Note the following example.

[7] Rush Welter, "The History of Ideas in America: An Essay in Redefinition," *The Journal of American History*, LI (March, 1965), p. 599.

[8] John W. Caughey, "Our Chosen Destiny," *Ibid.*, LII (September, 1965), p. 239.

The *ibid.* in the second footnote above refers to *The Journal of American History*. It could not have been used if an intervening footnote, referring to another periodical or book, had been present. It cannot refer to an author or title within a periodical itself. Remember that *ibid.* means "in the same place," i.e., the periodical, not the same work, which would refer to the article itself.

2. When no intervening reference occurs between a first full citation and the next reference to the same work, the footnote or footnotes may read *ibid.* The *ibid.* in this case stands for the name of the author, the title of the work, and the facts of publication. Note the following set of examples.

[5] Ray Billington, *Westward Expansion: A History of the American Frontier* (New York: The Macmillan Company, 1949), p. 113.

[6] *Ibid.*, p. 641.

[7] *Ibid.*, p. 532.

The second two footnotes above refer to different page numbers in *Westward Expansion*, and there has been no intervening reference to a different work.

If the writer chooses to use *ibid.*, he may also use the abbreviation *"op. cit.,"* which stands for *opere citato*, meaning "in the work cited." Whenever *ibid.* cannot be used because of an intervening reference to a different work, the surname of the author, followed by *op. cit.*, should be used. For example:

[5] Frederick Allen, *The Big Change* (New York: Harper & Row, Publishers, 1952), p. 86.

[6] William Ebenstein, *Modern Political Thought* (2nd ed.; New York: Holt, Rinehart and Winston, Inc., 1960), p. 465.

[7] Allen, *op. cit.*, p. 204.

In the event that only one work by the same author is being cited in a paper, there is no problem with the use of *op. cit.* But it could happen that more than one work by the same author is being used. Under such circumstances *op. cit.* would not really indicate to the reader which work was being cited. Thus, the shortened form technique would have to be used in such an instance.

Besides *op. cit.*, the abbreviation *"loc. cit.,"* standing for *loco citato*, "in the place cited," can be used under certain circumstances. If reference is being made to the *same page* and volume of a book or article previously cited, and intervening footnotes pertaining to different works have occurred thereby prohibiting the use of *ibid.*, the better abbreviation is *loc. cit.* rather than *op. cit.* This abbreviation is a little more specific than *op. cit.*, which refers only to a work in general. On the other hand, *loc. cit.* not only refers to a particular work but also stands for a specific place within that work. And obviously, under such a set of circumstances, no pagination is required in the footnote. It should be pointed out that *op. cit.* could be used in lieu of *loc. cit.*, but the volume number, if any, and the page number would have to be included.

Before proceeding to cite a list of different types of footnotes that illustrate all of the forms discussed, it would be well to caution the student in one respect: Footnotes are for the information of the reader. Whenever a work that has been fully cited is not referred to again for quite a number of pages and a number of other various references have intervened, it would be a good idea to repeat the citation in full because in all probability the reader has forgotten the original citation. With this in mind, many authors prefer to treat each chapter as if it were a new work for footnote purposes. All references are cited in full the first time they are used in a chapter, even though they may have been cited a number of times in the preceding chapter. Use of this technique means that readers will not be called upon to remember a particular complete citation for more than one chapter at the very most, and that they will not have to leaf back through the pages in search of the first full reference to the work in the event that they have forgotten it.

Sample Footnote Illustrations

[1] Albert K. Weinberg, *Manifest Destiny* (Baltimore: The Johns Hopkins Press, 1935), p. 109.

[2] *Ibid.*, p. 112. This view is further developed in Richard Van Alstyne, "International Rivalries in the Pacific Northwest," *Oregon Historical Quarterly*, XLVI (1945).

[3] Norman Graebner, *Empire on the Pacific* (New York: The Ronald Press, 1955), p. 961.

[4] Weinberg, *op. cit.*, p. 27.

[5] *Smith* v. *Turner*, 7 Howard 283 (1849).

[6] Graebner, *op. cit.*, p. 92.

[7] William E. Dodd, "The West and the War with Mexico," *Journal of the Illinois State Historical Society*, V (1912), p. 222.

[8] Oscar O. Winther, *The Old Oregon Country* (Stanford: The Stanford University Press, 1950), p. 990.

[9] Allan Nevins, *Fremont, The West's Greatest Adventurer* (2 vols.; New York: Harper and Brothers, 1928), I, p. 138.

[10] *Ibid.*, II, p. 708.

[11] Weinberg, *op. cit.*, p. 233.

[12] *Supra,* p. 13, footnote number 7.

[13] Bernard De Voto, *The Year of Decision 1846* (Boston: Houghton Mifflin, 1942), p. 91.

[14] *Loc. cit.*

[15] 16 *Stat.* 341.

[16] But this is only one legitimate viewpoint on the subject. Some writers would feel, as was indicated in Chapter VII, that land hunger was a more important factor.

[17] De Voto, *op. cit.*, p. 121.

[18] Otis A. Singletary, *The Mexican War* (Chicago: The University of Chicago Press, 1960), p. 300.

[19] *Ibid.*, p. 394.

[20] *Ibid.*, p. 100.

[21] Nevins, *op. cit.*, II, p. 400.

[22] Singletary, *op. cit.*, p. 268.

[23] James T. Adams, *The Epic of America* (Boston: Little, Brown, 1931), p. 197. See also the works cited *supra,* pp. 9, 17, 21, and 35.

The technique of placing all footnotes at the end of the work is an acceptable one; it eases the burden of both typist and publisher, but it imposes a rather serious hardship on readers who are consequently required to page back and forth through the work if they desire to check footnote references. As a result, the footnotes in such works quite often go unheeded by all except the truly conscientious student and scholar.

American Historiography

5

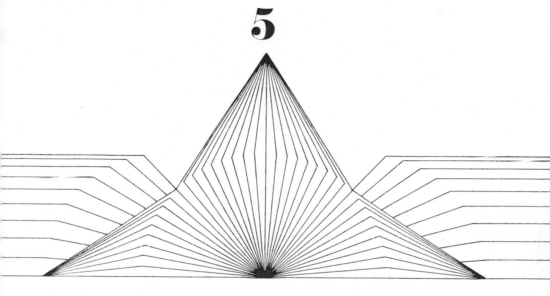

Whether making a selection for a book report or review, choosing works for inclusion in a term paper, or consulting works for an advanced research report, the student of history should possess a sound understanding and knowledge of the historiography of his or her field.

Historiography is the study of the various approaches to historical method, the actual writing of history, and, primarily, the various interpretations of historical events. Historiography is the study of the techniques employed by the individual historian. It is not necessary to study primary materials, i.e., original source materials, in order to study historiography. For historiography is concerned mainly with what has been written *about* historical events—the various schools of thought and interpretation centered around any particular historical occurrence—not with the source materials from which the historical fact was derived, although the methodology employed by the historian may be scrutinized to substantiate his or her conclusions. The primary sources of historiography are the works of historians.

History, especially American history, is often regarded as a cut-and-dried subject. But there are many significant, controversial topics in American history. These topics possess numerous legitimate, and sometimes conflicting, interpretations. The following is a partial list of the more controversial topics on which the interpretations of historians do not agree: causes for the various American wars, the handling of post-Civil War reconstruction, the evaluation of progressive Republicanism, considerations on the importance of the New Deal, the significance of the so-called Jeffersonian revolution, the importance of Jacksonian democracy, the role of the capitalist in the development of an industrialized America, the significance of the frontier experience, and so forth.

This chapter is concerned with tracing in outline form the development of American historiography. It should be emphasized, however, that the study of American historiography is a deep and penetrating subject, requiring a thorough knowledge not only of historical fact but of individual American historians as well.

Fortunately, several highly competent historians have at various times published detailed studies on the development of the writing of American history.[1] Also, the various national professional historical journals such as the *American Historical Review,* the *Journal of American History* (successor to the old *Mississippi Valley Historical Review*), plus the many regional, state, and specialized journals contain considerable information on this type of material.[2] A brief selection of historiographical articles may be found in the Bibliography, Appendix A.

1. The Foundation Period

In order to have the writing of an American history, a national consciousness had to be developed first. But the American nation, from the founding of Jamestown colony in 1607 to the close of the War of 1812 in December 1814, did not possess a true national consciousness. Consequently, the first historical-type writings in America reflected the prevailing English writing style carried over by the early settlers, i.e., they took the form of the literary essay.

[1] An excellent treatment is Michael Kraus, *The Writing of American History* (Norman: University of Oklahoma Press, 1953). See also William T. Hutchinson (ed.), *The Marcus W. Jernegan Essays in American Historiography* (Chicago: The University of Chicago Press, 1937); Hugh H. Bellot, *American History and American Historians* (London: The Athlone Press, 1952); Harvey Wish, *The American Historian: A Social-Intellectual History of the Writing of the American Past* (New York: Oxford University Press, 1960); George P. Gooch, *History and Historians in the 19th Century* (2nd ed.; London: Longmans, Green, 1913—Reprinted New York: Peter Smith, 1949); John S. Bassett, *The Middle Group of American Historians* (New York: The Macmillan Company, 1917); and most recently, John Higham, Leonard Krieger, and Felix Gilbert, *History* (Englewood Cliffs, New Jersey: Prentice-Hall, Inc., 1965).

[2] Special student subscription rates are available. Consult your instructor.

The American people had no history in the modern form we know today. John Smith's *A True Relation,* an account of the first year in Jamestown, written in 1608 is a case in point. Other colonial figures, such as William Bradford and John Winthrop, wrote similar colonial histories. Thus, for approximately the first one hundred fifty years of its experience, America had no real historical writing.

Nevertheless, throughout the colonial period a number of individuals kept diaries, wrote their memoirs, and composed local "histories," but these were either sporadic or provincial works, or both. They could hardly be termed historical writing.[3] The Revolutionary War, fortunately, provided the first significant spark of a national consciousness in the American people. Leading public figures such as Noah Webster and Benjamin Rush encouraged the people to write American history. In 1783, as a direct result of such efforts, the *Boston Magazine,* a journal devoted to the writing of the history of the Revolutionary War, made its appearance.

With this as a notable beginning, various other historical magazines also made their appearance throughout the 1780's forward. And some local historical societies were formed to perform the invaluable function of preserving and researching local history. The American nation produced some rather good, albeit provincial, state histories during the Revolutionary period. By way of example, Thomas Hutchinson wrote *A History of the Colony of Massachusetts Bay* shortly after the termination of the French and Indian War. Robert Proud wrote a *History of Pennsylvania* during the course of the Revolutionary War and published it afterwards. And Alex Hewat wrote a *History of South Carolina and Georgia* during the same period.

An individual named Parson Weems was also writing a great deal of material, which he very courageously and very optimistically referred to as history. But such was hardly the case. Weems was definitely not an historian: He was a propagandist for Americana, or better still he was a moralizer in the temper of medieval chroniclers. Not unlike a great many writers at a comparable stage in European historiography, Weems made an effort to romanticize —to sell to the American people—the idea of the American revolution and the new American nation. Weems both hero-worshipped to the point of idolatry and deliberately fabricated stories concerning the founders of the American republic. By way of illustration, he is responsible for the famous George Washington cherry tree story, which has, incidentally, absolutely no basis in historical

---

[3] See Kraus, *op. cit.,* Chapter II, for a very thorough account of American history writing in its formative stage.

fact. Historians are still fighting the widespread popular acceptance of the fiction of Weems and others like him. Still, Parson Weems was well read, and he did perform the notable function of helping to awaken a national consciousness in the American people.

At one point in American history an argument could be made for the need of this type of material to awaken a national consciousness in the people. When a national grouping does not possess its own heritage, it is forced to create one for its self-preservation. But this does not result in legitimate history writing. Today, however, the United States claims both a real history and a distinct national consciousness. It can solidly claim its fair share of legitimate heroes and bask in their exploits. It also possesses a constantly growing national heritage. Fabrication of historical fact serves no purpose; it has no place in historical writing now nor did it during the days of Parson Weems.

Fortunately, at the very time when Weems was writing his brand of "history," an American national consciousness was emerging. Whether or not his fictitious stories of American greatness contributed toward this development is begging the point. The fact is that it happened. Along with this development there occurred another development that was equally necessary for the formulation of a distinctively American school of historiography.

Before the actual writing of history can take place, research must be undertaken. Through patient, time-consuming research, primary source materials must be sought. This is both a very difficult and a lengthy process, with little in the way of tangible reward. The career researcher is above all a person of dedication (but by sheer accident he or she is sometimes rewarded financially—the exception to the rule). It is the good fortune of the American historical profession that during the first few decades of the nineteenth century a handful of such dedicated scholars began collecting and publishing historical documents. Examples of these collections include the Niles Collection (1822) on Revolutionary War materials; the Elliot Collection (1827–1830), which consists of five volumes of material on the constitutional debates; and above all, the Peter Force Collection, which consists of nine volumes of materials on the Revolutionary era, collected during the 1830's and the 1840's. Force's collection eventually became known as the American Archives.

The first really national history of the United States to be written by an American was a two-volume work by Timothy Pitkin in 1828, entitled *A Political and Civil History of the United States of America*. The work was rather weak when compared to modern surveys, but it did provide a beginning. Pitkin's real merit lies in the fact that he repudiated the prevailing provincialism and adopted a national outlook.

The first significant attempt by a European historian writing about the United States was a four-volume history by the Italian, Carlo Botta, entitled *A History of the War of Independence of the United States of America* (long titles were then in vogue), written in 1809. The fact that a European and not an American had written the first substantial history of the United States helped bring about an American interest in history writing. However, the works of Pitkin and Botta were of no lasting value, other than that they were pioneer works. Perhaps a more scholarly history of America was written by the German, Ebeling. Unfortunately, his seven-volume history, written during the first two decades of the nineteenth century, was composed in his native language, and as a result it was known only to very few Americans.

2. *The Romantic School*

The groundwork had been established for the development of the first truly distinguishable school of American historical writing. Known as the Romantic School, it predominated roughly from 1825 to 1880. Romantic history writing is characterized by general, voluminous works that were strictly narrative in form. They were not very factual or reliable, and these deficiencies were magnified by a near total absence of documented source materials. Concerned primarily with the chronicling of political events, romantic histories purposely idolized and romanticized American events and figures. If acts of stupendous courage were not known, and one had not been mentioned for several pages, one would be fabricated. Great stress was placed on individual feats of greatness, and American historians became as deeply entrenched in the "Great Man" approach as did their English contemporaries. Romantic histories also paid little heed to social and intellectual movements. Noted for their complete absence of objectivity and tolerence (in the pattern of twentieth-century nationalistic propaganda), they represented a very poor form of history writing.

But there was another side to the romantic period. For instance, during roughly the first half of the Romantic period, the name of Jared Sparks deserves mention. Sparks collected and published many volumes of Revolutionary era documents, notably the Washington papers, the Franklin papers, and volumes on revolutionary diplomatic correspondence. The number of volumes in this respect totals close to seventy.

Nevertheless, Sparks did exhibit some typical traits of the romantic historian. If he happened to discover a document that did not portray the American nation or one of its "heroes" in the most favorable light possible, he would not include it in his published collection. Hence, his work was both biased and loaded with errors; he did not utilize good historical methodology. Despite these shortcomings, however, the efforts of Jared Sparks resulted in a tremendous contribution to American documentary collections. And fortunately, later, more objective historians who made use of these documents were able to uncover and correct most of his errors.

The leader of the Romantic School of American historians, and the reputed father of American history writing, is the Transcendentalist, George Bancroft. He wrote a voluminous history of the United States, with the discovery of the American continent as his starting point. Planning to survey the entire period of American history, Bancroft became bogged down in his beloved Revolutionary period and never completed his projected task. He did, however, add two more volumes during the 1880's, but he was still considerably short of his anticipated objective. It might also be added that romantic history writing was no longer in vogue by this time.

Bancroft's writings contain a curious mixture of good historical method, the prevailing hero worship, a zealous advocacy of both providence and progress views of history, and the thesis that the American nation was divinely inspired to lead the world to a democratic utopia under American dominance. The preface to his work very aptly stated his theme, and it is interesting reading for any student in an American history class. In spite of its obvious drawbacks, when Bancroft's first volume appeared in 1834 it was hailed as the beginning of a distinctively American school of historical writing, and American history writing became fairly well established.

A notable exception to the Romantic School of history writing during its period of dominance was Richard Hildreth. Making the first really significant attempt to avoid the prevailing hero worship theme, Hildreth succeeded quite well. Unfortunately, Hildreth was still guilty of being nonobjective. His writing was most definitely pro-Federalist, but it was nonetheless far superior to the other writings during the period. His six-volume history was written during the years 1849–1851 and carried the story of America from the settling of the continent up through the Compromise of 1821.

The contributions of the Romantic School of American Historians were of an indirect nature. They instilled the American

people with an intense patriotism for their nation—a patriotism
that did not exist in any large measure before the romantics picked
up their pens. Although beneficial to the growth of America, this
patriotic achievement on the part of the Romantic School historians is not the function of legitimate history. But while writing
their highly propagandized version of the past, the romantics were,
in the process, creating the proper climate for the establishment of
modern historical objectivity. By generating an interest in history
they nurtured the development of an historical sense that would
eventually destroy the romanticized history they were authoring.

A transitional figure, one who pointed the way toward a
change in historical writing, was Francis Parkman. His many volumes were published between 1851–1892. Following the literary
rather than the historical narrative style, Parkman nonetheless
wrote some classic American history in a most interesting and refreshing manner. He succeeded at times in making accurately portrayed history read like a novel. The history profession could use
many more such stylists as Francis Parkman.

3. The Scientific School

History writing, in the modern sense, was established around
1880 with the development of the Scientific School of American
historians. To a large extent based on the style, methodology, and
philosophy of the great German scientific historian, Leopold von
Ranke, the Scientific School of history writing provided the basis
for modern day historical techniques.

Led by such notables as Andrew White, Daniel Gilman, and
Henry Adams, the American Scientific School of historical writing
and inquiry possessed many worthwhile and distinguishing characteristics. First, it demanded accuracy in quotations, and this resulted in the quoting of exact statements. Second, it insisted on
accurate documentation and a copious quantity of footnotes.
Third, the Scientific School gave political history its just consideration, but it also took into account social, cultural, and economic
history as well, embracing a much broader perspective than did the
preceding Romantic School. Fourth, Scientific School historians,
at least during the pioneer stages of the movement, completely
ignored previous authors. In an attempt to insure historical accuracy they returned to the original sources for their information.
Fifth, the Scientific School was characterized by a considerable
amount of debunking—this tendency was also extremely popular
during the 1920's. Thus, scientific historians exhibited a tempo-
rary tendency to be cynical, and the old heroes of the romantic

period, if their heroism had no basis in historical fact, began to topple. A principal achievement for an early scientifically oriented historian was to solidly establish himself in the profession by destroying some false heroic image.

And finally, the scientific historian, as the name implies, regarded history as something of a science, in that facts were to be reasonably proven, not assumed. Great stress was placed on the methodology of historical research and writing. As a consequence, the scientific-minded historian soon became quite concerned with the proper training of future historians. Having expended considerable efforts in this concern, the Scientific School was responsible for history becoming a respectable graduate school endeavor, and the study of history achieving full-time professional status. For along with Von Ranke's methodology came the German educational structure, and the Scientific School advocates adopted Von Ranke's seminar technique, the German graduate research degree system, and the detailed graduate study of history in the American educational system.[4] These developments were just a part of the German-influenced educational revolution that took place in the United States during the 1880's.

In an effort to further "professionalize" their new disciplinary status, the Scientific School historians organized professional societies and began publishing professional journals. The American Historical Association was founded in 1884, and it inaugurated the *American Historical Review* in 1895. The Mississippi Valley Historical Association was founded in 1907 and shortly afterwards began the publication of the *Mississippi Valley Historical Review*. Originally a regional organization, it gradually broadened in scope, and within a few decades it became a national organization in every way except in name. In 1965, in recognition of this long-standing development, the Mississippi Valley Historical Association officially changed its name to the Organization of American Historians and the name of its publication to *The Journal of American History*.

These were notable developments, but there was a more important one. Above all else, the scientific historian made every possible attempt to be objective in the interpretation of historical fact. This characteristic is without a doubt the scientific historian's most noteworthy contribution to the discipline of history. Outstanding examples of scientific-minded historians who were pioneers in the objective orientation are Edward Channing and Henry Adams.

---

[4] Bear these characteristics of critical or scientific history in mind when we discuss European historiography in the next chapter.

With the advent of the Scientific School and its various characteristics, the American historian began to specialize in a particular area or period. This development quickly gave rise to a number of schools of interpretation and emphasis within the framework of the new scientific method.

NATIONALIST SCHOOL   Historically, the first such Scientific School of specialization to arise was the Nationalist School of historical interpretation. The nationalistic historians upheld as their key tenet the idea that the development of a strong nation-state should be the major objective of any people. Hence, they displayed a marked tendency to deify the nation. Writing primarily during the Age of Big Business, the nationalists equated national progress with individual material prosperity. They had a very high regard for property rights, and consequently they adopted a rather conservative approach to change.

A list of noted nationalistic historians would include: John B. McMaster, who introduced studies of the "common man" in his volumes and thereby paved the way for the eventual development of American social history; and James Rhodes, John Burgess, and John Fiske (Fiske upheld the "white man's burden" theory). Incidentally, when McMaster began his studies of the common man, the so-called Great Man approach to the study of history began to decline.

INTERNATIONALIST SCHOOL   Arising in part to counteract the nationalists and in part to achieve an even greater degree of objectivity (the nationalists were avowedly partisan) were the internationalists, also known as the imperialists—a term subject to misinterpretation. Adherents of this school refused to regard the United States as being strictly "American" and stressed the fact that America was at one time British. Like the nationalists, the internationalists also favored their own nation, but being more objective, they were willing to acknowledge the tremendous influences that Great Britain in particular and Europe in general rendered to the development of the United States. These historians possessed a much wider perspective than did their nationalistic contemporaries. As a consequence, they were able to write their histories of the colonial period in a much more objective manner. Notable examples of internationalist historians are George Beer, Herbert Osgood, and Lawrence Gipson.

SECTIONALIST SCHOOL   While nationalists and internationalists were conducting a battle over the origins and nature of the American nation, a third fragment of the Scientific School developed. In the absence of a better term, we might allude to this third group as the regionalists or sectionalists. Highly conscious of the complexities of American life and culture, the sectionalists believed that by thoroughly investigating the history of a particular region they could gain further insight into the American nation as a whole. The sectionalist school was originally a western school, for this section of the country—the frontier—was obviously and traditionally the most "national" type section of the nation in character. Therefore, its character undoubtedly exerted great influence on the national character—at least, this was the primary assumption of this school.

This western sectionalistic school, better known as the Frontier School, produced some very prominent American historians. Hubert H. Bancroft, for instance, wrote some twenty-eight volumes on the Far West and collected tens of thousands of documents. Reuben G. Thwaites wrote well over one hundred volumes, primarily on western travel and Jesuit missionary activity. Herbert E. Bolton concentrated on the Spanish borderlands—that geographical area where Anglo, Latin, and Indian cultures met and clashed. This subject, incidentally, is a very rich field for investigation.

But by far the biggest name among these giant-sized western sectional historians is that of Frederick Jackson Turner. According to the "Turner thesis," the frontier experience, coupled with American expansion into an area of free land, molded the character and institutions of modern day America. The Turnerite interpretation is gradually losing its influence; a modern but moderate exponent is the well-known historian, Ray Allen Billington.

Prompted by the successes of the westerners, other historians began to concentrate on other portions of the country. Ulrich B. Phillips and William E. Dodd wrote extensively on southern contributions to the American nation. Samuel E. Morison and James T. Adams did likewise for New England.

THE CULTURAL SCHOOL   At the very time when the sectionalists were making their big push, a fourth fragmentation of the Scientific School was in the making. For lack of a better term, and fully admitting to its probable deficiencies, let us refer to this school as the Cultural School. The word "cultural" will be used in its broadest possible sense. It is very difficult to give this school an adequate label. Some historians refer to it as the "New History," but the movement is broader than a sociological-integrated approach to interpretation that the New History advocates. The group of historians who belong to the Cultural School emphasizes various areas of human behavior and the effect of this behavior on the development of American society.

The Cultural School was given major impetus by Dixon Ryan Fox and Arthur M. Schlesinger with their thirteen-volume *A His-*

tory of American Life, begun in 1928, which was an attempt to integrate and correlate the various social sciences in an effort to better understand and interpret the human past. Cultural historians choose specific topics of personal interest, e.g., literature, economics, folklore, philosophy, and sociology, and then write the histories of these subjects and indicate their influence on the development of American ideas, attitudes, and practices.

One extremely influential historian who fits into this grouping is Charles Beard. In his "Economic Interpretations" of the formation of the Constitution and of the Jeffersonian era, Beard's view was that economic factors have shaped American institutions, government, and subsequent developments. He synthesized historical fact and economic principles in an effort to explain the past. Beard was careful to point out, however, that economic motives alone did not explain America, just as Turner indicated that more than the frontier experience was required to create the American character.

The advocates of both men, the "Beardians" and the "Turnerians," were and oftentimes are too zealous. The disciples quite often push the thesis of their masters further than was originally intended, causing some very interesting and colorful battles between the adherents of the various schools of interpretation. Any historical thesis should be accepted strictly for what it is—a thesis. The formulators of theses are usually more prone to admit probable deficiencies in their theories than are their disciples.

MODERN TRENDS Some modern historians still belong to either the Turner or the Beard school, but the theses of both historians have been attacked and criticized from many quarters. There is a growing number of historians who, in the tradition of Fox and Schlesinger, pursue the integrated cultural aspect of the American experience. Partially triggered by James Harvey Robinson's lectures on European intellectual history at Columbia and his subsequent development of the "New History," these historians include Vernon Parrington, Ralph Gabriel, and Merle Curti. Such historians emphasize the role and importance of ideas, culture, and social institutions in attempting to explain the United States.

This "intellectual" approach to the study of history, which is a movement within the Cultural School, has resulted in a number of notable developments on the contemporary scene. Several programs in American Studies, emphasizing an integration of history with literature, philosophy, and other related disciplines, have been initiated. The Ph.D. degree, which traditionally has reflected training in research techniques and scholarship, is also the standard, academic credential for university teaching and is being conferred, for example, in the "History of Ideas" and the "History of Science."

The intellectual approach is an extremely difficult one in that it presupposes not only a thorough grounding in history but a rather detailed mastery of one or more other related disciplines as well. It is a thoroughly integrated approach to the human past.

A pioneer in the intellectual area was Dixon Ryan Fox, whose *Ideas in Motion* provided major impetus for the movement. *The Growth of American Thought,* authored by Merle Curti, is a monumental, Pulitzer-Prize-winning study on the subject. Other historians—notably the late Richard Hofstadter and the late Clinton Rossiter—attempted to explain American political behavior in terms of the growth and development of particular ideologies. Theirs was an intellectual approach to history. Other prominent members of the school include William Cash, Perry Miller, and Loren Baritz. The area of intellectual history is fertile ground for new and refreshing studies on the American nation.

Various historians have attempted to discover the basic factors of human behavior by discovering "laws" and by emphasizing economic factors, geographical factors, etc. Throughout the twentieth century there has been a growing tendency to interpret past human behavior in terms of the disciplines of human behavior, *viz.,* sociology and psychology, particularly the former.

The sociological approach to historical interpretation is reflective of Robinson's "New History," even though Robinson himself emphasized the need for the wide integration of factors in historical study rather than a detailed application of sociological principles alone. The key to the approach is an emphasis on the role of environment in shaping human actions. Hence, a knowledge of social evolution and the principles of social organization must become part of the working tools of the professional historian. Max Weber and Karl Lamprecht are early examples of German scholars who employed this technique.

Moving further into the twentieth century, some historians are beginning to concentrate on a slightly different factor—motivation. An analysis of the motivation of the characters on the historical stage has become extremely important in formulating an intelligent appraisal of the human past. With this development there occurs an increasing concern for the utilization of the scientific apparatus of sociology, and for the methodology and theorizing of psychology.

Real impetus for new techniques (which find their origins in the World War II era) resulted from a series of lectures given by the late historian, David M. Potter, at the University of Chicago in 1950. These lectures emphasized the contributions of the behavioral scientist to an interpretation of the American character and pleaded for the utilization of behavioral techniques in historical inquiry. The ideas which Potter put forth found practical application in his *People of Plenty.*

Building upon the base established by Potter is C. G. Hempel. He introduced the use of a model of social systems against which suspected historical laws or patterns would be tested. J. S. Bruner added the use of concept analysis to the working tools of the "behavioral historian."[5]

The behavioral approach as it is applied to political science, i.e., the statistical approach that employs the theory of games, bloc behavior patterns, and other devices, does not find direct application to most aspects of history. However, the behavioral findings of political scientists and sociologists can and do add to the reservoir of fact utilized by historians in their interpretations.

Unfortunately, a work occasionally appears that attempts to apply the techniques of psychology to an historical figure, as if that figure were currently pouring out his or her soul to a skilled psychiatrist. When working with a live subject the psychiatrist is often unable to pinpoint difficulties. The problem is compounded tremendously when one tries to perform motivational analysis on someone who has been dead for decades or centuries. This approach does not constitute good historical inquiry, nor is it a legitimate behavioral approach.[6]

The proper application of the behavioral technique is quite difficult. Some historians will not accept it, claiming that it destroys history as a distinct discipline and makes it subsidiary to sociology or some other "social science." Consequently, "behavioral" historians must exercise great care in making a distinction between description and explanation in their use of such tools. They properly use them to *explain* the behavior of their characters; sociologists, on the other hand, utilize a descriptive technique. They are interested in institutions as they evolve into the present scheme of things, whereas historians are concerned with these same institutions only as they affect their characters and provide adequate explanations for past behavior.

Modern day America, in large measure, is a computerized society. High speed computers can scan millions of data in minutes and interpret, arrange, or select these data in whatever manner they have been programmed for by researchers. The "pure" sci-

[5]See N. L. Gage (ed.), *Handbook of Research on Teaching* (Chicago: Rand McNally and Company, 1963) and Benjamin B. Wolman (ed.), *The Psychoanalytic Interpretation of History* (New York: Basic Books, 1971).

[6]One of the recent works, which has been widely criticized by historians in published reviews, is Sigmund Freud and William C. Bulleit, *Thomas Woodrow Wilson: Twenty-Eighth President of the United States, A Psychological Study* (Boston: Houghton Mifflin Company, 1967).

ences very quickly observed the advantages of computers and utilized them for research. Some of the social sciences, especially political science, economics, and sociology, soon followed suit. And quite recently the computer has given rise to the Quantitative School of historical research.[7]

The great advantage of computer-aided historical inquiry is that it allows researchers to obtain insights into vast numbers of people rather than a few select individuals. Computers force their proponents to employ a very rigorous scientific method; they must systematize procedures, formulate hypotheses, break down data into minute parts, and convert their theory or problem into a computer language. A leading quantitative exponent in political history is Paul Kleppner; in social history, Rudy Ray Seward; in the relatively new field of urban history, Howard Chudacoff, Gordon W. Kirk, Jr., and Stephan Thernstrom; and in economic history, H. James Henderson, James B. Rhoads, Barbara Fisher, Robert W. Fogel, and Stanley L. Engerman. Of all quantitative studies to date, perhaps Fogel and Engerman's controversial *Time on the Cross: The Economics of American Negro Slavery* (1974) has focused the greatest deal of attention on the methodology, assumptions, hypotheses, and techniques of quantitative historians.

Modern historians are definitely not agreed on the value of computers for historical inquiry. The great debate is over what some historians see as the dehumanization of history. It does not appear likely that large numbers of historians will employ the quantitative approach even if they possess the desire to do so. The high cost of computer use, the general lack of technical training on the part of historians, and the absence of data in a form suitable for computer use will prevent a widespread movement to quantified history in the foreseeable future. There have been, however, a number of consortia and societies established in recent years to disseminate knowledge about computer-aided research.

Historians should maintain an open mind toward all approaches, methods, and mechanical apparatus that might be of aid to their inquiry. Only objective investigation can determine whether or not new technology is advantageous to the study of history. Current trends in American historical research should prove highly fruitful in the near future.

---

[7]See Edward Shorter, *The Historian and the Computer: A Practical Guide* (Englewood Cliffs: Prentice-Hall, 1971); Roderick Floud, *An Introduction to Quantitative Methods for Historians* (Princeton: Princeton University Press, 1973); and Robert P. Swierenga, "Computers and American History: The Impact of the 'New' Generation," *The Journal of American History*, Vol. LX, No. 4 (March, 1974).

Questions For Discussion

1.   What are the characteristics of the Romantic School of American historiography?

2.   Which period of American historical writing has been the most effective? To what extent is this question a relative consideration?

3.   What are the contributions to historical understanding produced by cultural and intellectual historians?

4.   In what respects may the quantitative approach to history be advantageous to historical inquiry? Are there any drawbacks to the quantitative approach?

5.   What are the major characteristics of scientific historical writing? How are they in evidence in the contemporary era?

European Historiography

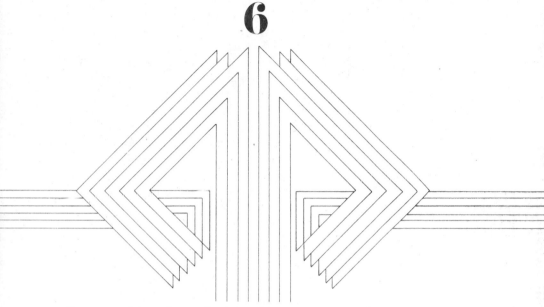

6

European historiography constitutes an extremely complex study, especially when compared with American historiography, owing to the vast time period involved—some 2500 years. Obviously, some sweeping generalizations will have to be made in order to survey this material in a single chapter, for entire books have been written on particular phases of European historiography.

Another reason for the complexity of European historiography is the vast number of countries involved. It cannot be hoped to detail here the development of historiography for all of the nations that appeared and disappeared during the course of European history. This chapter will concentrate primarily on the historiography of the major countries of Europe and only mention the other countries whenever generalized observations are possible.[1]

[1] For detailed reading see James W. Thompson and Bernard J. Holm, *A History of Historical Writings* (2 vols.; New York: The Macmillan Company, 1942); Bernadotte E. Schmitt, *Some Historians of Modern Europe* (Chicago: The University of Chicago Press, 1942); George P. Gooch, *History and Historians in the 19th Century* (New York: Longmans, Green, 1948); James T. Shotwell, *The History of History,* Vol. I (New York: Columbia University Press, 1939); Harry E. Barnes, *A History of Historical Writing* (2nd rev. ed.; New York: Dover Publications, Inc., 1963); Matthew A. Fitzsimons, Alfred G.

1. Greco-Roman Historical Writing

Probably the pioneer historian in the Western world was Homer, but by modern standards the epic themes of the *Iliad* and the *Odyssey* could hardly be considered good history.[2] Homer did give us some of the history of his age, and subsequent writers transformed the Homerian epic into the narrative form—the style used today. But in terms of objectivity and tolerance, early Greek writers were unable to divorce themselves from their gods, and consequently much of their history is legend and myth. They are important for the fact that they provided an acceptable writing form for historical inquiry.

Upon this base Herodotus wrote his famous *History of the Persian Wars*. He viewed these wars as a clash between two different cultures and felt it necessary to delve into an explanation of these cultures. Attempting to be objective, he gave due credit to the hated Persians for their accomplishments. Because of this, and despite the weaknesses in Greek historical interpretation brought on by the widespread acceptance of gods, myth, and legend in their historical writings, Herodotus has been commonly regarded as the "father of history."

Building upon Herodotus was Thucydides, who wrote a history of the Peloponnesian War. Thucydides was the first true historian in that he sought to assess causes, insisted upon accuracy, and attained a fair degree of objectivity. Of equal importance was his insistence on the utility of historical study for coping with future, similar problems. His major weakness was an overemphasis on political matters, and as a result, Thucydides unknowingly established a pattern that remained quite strong until the nineteenth century, *viz.*, the dominating concern for political issues in historical writing.

Perhaps this development, which was due to the insistence of Thucydides on utility, also caused Greek history writing to lose much of its flavor over the next few centuries. The writings of later historians were undertaken primarily to instruct the reader in moral principles, and historical technique was allowed to suffer. But Polybius restored the tradition of Herodotus and Thucydides in his history of the Punic Wars era, and again, accuracy, objectivity, and utility were jointly emphasized.

Pundt, and Charles E. Nowell (eds.), *The Development of Historiography* (Harrisburg, Pennsylvania: The Stackpole Company, 1954); and S. William Halperin, *Some Twentieth-Century Historians* (New York: Alfred A. Knopf, Inc., 1961).

[2]The authenticity of much of Homer's *Odyssey*, however, is interestingly presented in Ernle Bradford, *Ulysses Found* (New York: Harcourt, Brace & World, 1963).

Early Roman history was strongly influenced by the preceding Greek history. The first Roman historian, Pictor (ca. 250 B.C.), wrote his account of the Punic Wars in the Greek language. The first Roman historian to write in Latin was Cato, a half-century later.

A major popularizer of Roman history writing was Julius Caesar. His *Commentaries on the Gallic Wars* and his later *Commentaries on the Civil War* emphasized objectivity, clarity, and a high degree of accuracy, even though Caesar wrote primarily to establish his own reputation. A contemporary writer, Sallust, was important in that he attempted to assess the character and the values of the aristocracy. Thus his work tended toward the moralistic—but Polybius had long before stated that the historian must make value judgments.

The name of Livy is important in any consideration of Roman historiography. Unfortunately, Livy was not greatly concerned with accuracy and objectivity. He wrote with the obvious intent of selling Rome to the Romans (a Roman equivalent to Parson Weems?). But Livy did succeed in giving the modern historian a rather clear insight into the spirit and times of the early Romans.

The next and last great figure in Roman historiography was Tacitus, who died around 120 A.D. Employing some of the scientific techniques exemplified by Polybius, Tacitus in his famous *Annals* and *Histories* attempted to give an impartial account of the decline of Roman greatness. Yet his personal prejudices were obvious. His real strength was his ability to analyze the political intrigue that characterized his age. In another work, more sociological than historical, *Germania,* Tacitus gave the world its best account of the Teutonic movement into imperial Rome.

Some generalizations on Greco-Roman historiography can now be attempted. There was some progress being made in the development of historical writing and technique. Most historians at least tried to be accurate and objective in their work. The main deficiency of the historians of the ancient world was the influence of the gods, myth, and undocumented legend that continually crept into their writings. Nonetheless, the crude essentials for the rigorous writing of history were established.

2. Early Christian Historical Writing

Christianity brought an abrupt change to the tenor of historical writing; unfortunately, it was a retrogressive change. The works of the Greek and Roman historians were largely spurned. After all, they were the products of pagan minds. This close-

minded attitude naturally resulted in another detrimental effect
on history. Early Christian writers were openly and avowedly not
objective. Not only were they hostile to any achievement by a
pagan culture, but their interpretations were slanted in such a
manner so as to make Christianity appear as favorable as possible,
even to the point of bending or overlooking facts in order to do so.
In this respect, early Christian writers, e.g., Eusebius and Jerome,
offered nothing of importance to historical writing.

However, early Christian authors did make contributions to
the discipline of history in other respects. Augustine's *City of God,*
unlike the works of the pagans, proposed an end (teleological view)
for history, whereas the pagans had been content with a cyclical
interpretation. Thus, Christian historians formulated the first real
philosophy of history.[3] Early Christians also sought to establish
a longstanding heritage for their beliefs in an effort to attract converts to their religion. This they were able to do through the use of
the Old Testament as an historical document. But in order to indicate a continuity between Hebrew and Christian thought, they
found it necessary to develop chronologies of the past. Thus, it
came about that the *Chronicles* of Jerome, a translation and ampli-
fication of an earlier work by Eusebius, became the basis for chronological reckoning in the Western world, a system that lasted well
into modern times.

With the fall of Roman civilization in the West in 476 A.D., the
first distinguishable school of European historiography made its
appearance. The medieval period had begun, and Europe, as we
commonly regard it, was beginning to evolve.

3. Medieval Historiography

In general, medieval historians combined theology and historical fact to produce their widespread interpretation of a providen-
tially inspired course of human events. Material developments were
given scant attention. This was to be expected in view of the fact
that most medieval historians were Christian monks. These men
tended to reshape historical fact, if deemed necessary, in order to
present their religious beliefs in the best possible light. This does
not mean to imply that these writers deliberately deceived their
readers. So sincerely and thoroughly were they convinced of the
validity of their beliefs that in most instances they were unable
even to approach objectivity.

[3]The reader is referred to the sections on cyclical and providential philosophies of
history in Chapter 3.

Cause-and-effect relationships were poorly handled by the early medievalists. An intervening providence was the easiest and most generally used explanation for any given historical happening. And the works of the pagan historians, regardless of their factual merits, received very little perusal, except to illustrate the presence of the forces of evil in the world.

An important representative figure of the early medieval period was Gregory of Tours, the author of *History of the Franks*. As a history, Gregory's work leaves much to be desired, but it does provide us with our only detailed account of the Merovingian Period. Gregory, as well as other churchmen-authors of the period, emphasized the role of the Church in its society. His work contains numerous allusions to miracles, not to mention a sermonic quality. But what made Gregory popular was the fact that he wrote in vernacular Latin, a writing form more readily understood by a larger number of people. Venerable Bede, the author of *Ecclesiastical History of the English People*, wrote in the same temper, but Bede tended to play down the role of miracles in history and attempted to be more judicious in choosing his source materials.

Moving into the ninth century—the period of the Carolingian Renaissance—the writing of history began an upward sweep. Any further consideration of European historiography must take into account the existence of various national groupings. Charlemagne commenced a revival of letters; and history, including a consideration of the pagan historians of the ancient world, became a part of the Carolingian educational structure.

Charlemagne required the various monasteries in his realm to keep accurate records. Consequently, monks made rather cryptic notations on what of importance happened during a particular season or year. These "annals" as they were called, consisted of straightforward report accounts; they rarely contained any interpretation or comment. One could not ask for greater objectivity or for a more valuable source of factual information about the medieval period, although much was left to be desired in terms of an interesting writing style.

In most instances these annals were combined, expanded with some additional fact or a bit of interpretation, and called chronicles. In many cases a chronicle was a very provincial work. It would cover the "history" of a particular monastery or town. But over a period of approximately two centuries, these chronicles began to develop into something approaching historical writing. The *Chronicle* of Otto of Freising (see below) in the twelfth century was indicative of this new tendency. The development of annals and chronicles comprised the outstanding events of early medieval historiography.

Beginning with the eleventh century, considerable change was taking place. Europe, reintroduced to the ancient Near East through the Crusades and to a new "pagan" group, the Vikings, was beginning to pay a little more attention to secular matters. Also instrumental in effecting this change in attitude was the growing number of political difficulties as Europe was beginning to develop into distinct nations. As a consequence, even though churchmen were still responsible for most historical writing, outside pressures were forcing them to give considerably more attention to secular matters.

There were no full-time historians during the Middle Ages, and history was not offered as a distinct discipline in the rising university. History remained, as in the Carolingian period, a part of the subject matter of grammar. There were no attempts to standardize the writing format or the methodology of history. No real attempt was made to delve into the past, for most historians were primarily concerned with their own times. They were content with providing some sort of a record of their own age, along with some general instructions on morality.

Otto of Freising characterizes medieval historiographic study. Although careless in the handling of details, he did make use of reliable sources; and his work is considered important by modern medievalists. Yet since Otto was a bishop, he was biased against secular affairs and thereby employed a moralistic slant in his interpretations. Nonetheless, Otto did make an attempt to consider causes and effects. Unfortunately, his religious office partially blinded him from an objective analysis of the secular world.

Moving into the later Middle Ages, increasing attention was being given to record keeping and document collecting. Many feudal lords began employing clerks, and as a result, more detailed chronicles were being compiled. As time passed, these chronicles became broader in scope and provided the future historian worthwhile tools with which to reconstruct the past.

4. Renaissance Historiography

The period of the Renaissance was an era of renewed interest in antiquity, the classics, and literary criticism. It was an age when the study of humankind became important; it was an age of secularization. Consequently, the Renaissance era produced some notable developments in the field of historiography.

The interest in antiquity resulted in the writing of history from a less provincial viewpoint. No longer were historians simply the chroniclers of their own times; the past began to find a place in historical writing and inquiry. Pagan histories were being studied and imitated. The result was greater concern for secular activities. Writers became more critical of their own works and the works of others. The convenient utilization of an intervening providence to explain human affairs was giving way somewhat to a determination of proximate and remote causation. Above all, the true humanistic historian desired truth.

But truth was not always present. History still was not a full-time profession. Writers required patrons in order to support their work. Oftentimes the historical works of these writers made the patron, whether individual or institution, a little more likeable than the facts would warrant. Renaissance writers of history had not yet placed proper emphasis on historical objectivity.

Nonetheless, interest in historical studies was improving tremendously. Interest in the classics resulted in the feverish search for the lost manuscripts of antiquity, and some individuals collected and published documents and sources. Publishing, of course, was aided considerably by the invention of the printing press, a decided boon for the destruction of the old provincialism, which was slowly being replaced by an emphasis on nationalism.

The father of Renaissance history writing, or humanism as the literary style was termed, was Francesco Petrarch (1304–1374). Petrarch wrote on the civilizations of the ancient classical era and succeeded in debunking some of the myths dealing with the Roman period. Although he did not utilize good historical method, he did champion interest in historical study. And this interest was no better witnessed than in Florence, one area in the Italies with a civilization conducive to the development of historical works. Hence, near the end of the Italian Renaissance, Machiavelli (1469–1527) performed real yoeman service in determining causes for historical events. Machiavelli marked the change-over from a providential to a definite, secular orientation in history. He also stressed the need for historical study in explaining political affairs, thus giving history a definite, practical application.

Beyond the Italies the influence of the Renaissance was felt later. Of particular importance was Jean Bodin, a Frenchman who wrote the first major work on historical method. In this work, *Method for the Easy Comprehension of History*, Bodin emphasized the need for proper interpretation of source materials and placed major stress on geographical factors in shaping human events.

While the Renaissance was bringing about the aforementioned changes in historiography, the Reformation rocked the unity of medieval Christendom. Historical writing, except for the concurrent humanistic movement, became involved in the religious controversies of the day. For a time history again dwelt on theology; it was characterized by a moralistic spirit quite similar to that of the early Middle Ages.

5. Reformation Historiography

The writing of history became the writing of propaganda during the Reformation era. Objectivity was temporarily forgotten. History became purely utilitarian; its purpose was to sway converts to either the Catholic or the Protestant point of view. A good result of this propagandism, however, was the penetrating search for historical documents, even though the motivation of the document seekers was far from commendable. Catholics sought to prove beyond any doubt, on the basis of historical fact, that Protestantism was the anti-Christ. And Protestants were equally convinced that Catholics were the agents of the devil. Both camps sought to add respectability and credence to their positions by adequate documentation. As a result, a considerable number of heretofore unknown historical documents were discovered and published.

Among Protestant historians a favorite device was to point out the cruelty of Catholic persecutions. John Foxe, in *The Acts and Monuments of the Christian Martyrs* (1563), definitely portrayed this theme. The *Magdeburg Centuries,* edited by Flacius, monumentally surveyed the story of Christianity with the planned intent of proving that the Church of Rome had deliberately subverted true Christianity. Another prominent historian among the Protestants was Phillip Milanchthon, but more objective was John Knox, one of the few Reformation era polemicists to present the historical facts in a reasonably honest manner. The work of Sleidanus is also worthy of mention, not for his contribution to the Protestant cause, but rather for his indirect contributions to the discipline of history. Sleidanus made ample use of original historical documents and other works to emphasize political factors as causes for the Reformation.

The Catholic counterattack was very ably led by Baronius, whose *Ecclesiastical Annals* outrivals the *Magdeburg Centuries* in venom. Baronius collected a vast number of documents but judiciously used only those which furthered the Catholic cause. Such deception, common among polemicists in both camps, could hardly be termed good history. Another supporter of the Catholic cause, Bossuet, wrote without the passions of his contemporaries. A definite partisan, he nonetheless attempted a degree of objectivity uncommon in his chaotic age. He also presented one of the last pleas for a providential view of historical interpretation.

6. Rationalist Historiography

During the time when Europe was embroiled in religious controversy, foreboding changes in other realms were in the making. This was due primarily to Europe's geographical and intellectual expansion. Columbus, Da Gama, Magellan, and Hudson were discovering the size and scope of the world, while individuals such as Richard Hakluyt popularized their findings. Intellectual giants of the caliber of Galileo, Descartes, and Newton were laying the groundwork for a veritable revolution in intellectual thought and attitude.

Descartes had succeeded in wiping out the philosophical authoritarianism of the past; the human mind was now free to doubt anything. And the Newtonian World Machine provided an order to the universe that had been unknown since the beginning of time. Laws of nature were within the grasp of human knowledge. People needed only faith in themselves to achieve tremendous wonders. John Locke suggested a new philosophy based on empirical observation (sense perception), and the Frenchman, Fontenelle, predicted continued progress for humanity.

These developments made possible an intellectual climate ripe for the formation of some notable advances in historical writing. One of the most worthwhile characteristics of this change in attitude was a marked tendency to broaden the scope of historical study. The resultant Rationalist School of historical writing considered the social, cultural, and economic aspects of human endeavor as well as the traditional theological and political aspects of the subject.

In keeping with the prevailing Enlightenment philosophy this school of history writing emphasized the human intellect as the decisive factor in human developments rather than the old providential notion. Another Enlightenment belief, that environment shapes human behavior, also influenced historical writing. Hence, historians emphasized climate, geography, and social and political institutions in attempting to explain human behavior. There was a definite humanitarian thread running throughout rationalistic works.

The Enlightenment produced new developments in historiography. Rationalist history was marked by attempts to write world or "universal" histories, giving rise to periodization. The Dutchman, Cellarius, divided history into ancient, medieval, and new periods. Although rationalistic historians attempted to be objective, they wrote with a definite end in mind. Historical fact always proves, according to their interpretation, that humankind advances whenever the human race is not being tyrannized. This insistence on a progress view of history was one of the biggest characteristics of the school.

Giambattista Vico (1668–1744) was representative of this belief. In his writings the old notion of a gradually declining culture is replaced by the continuous development of processes that bring about the steady progress of humanity. And in such a frame of reference, miracles become unnecessary in justifying history. Natural laws are considered far better. Vico devised a spiral-type progress: Society is moving in cycles, but they are upward-moving cycles. Interestingly enough, Vico and his progress-believing contemporaries were taking a conservative approach to progress because they could not anticipate the enormous technological and scientific advances that soon came about. The most widely attributed cause for the lack of progress in the past had been the alleged tyrannical nature of authoritarian religion; most early progress-believers attacked organized religion.

The most prominent of all rationalist historians was Edward Gibbon (1737–1794), whose classic *The History of the Decline and Fall of the Roman Empire* is still widely read. Gibbon's work is characterized by good style and organization, a very accurate portrayal of facts, and a popular theme. He enjoyed a great reputation among his contemporaries as well as among modern historians. Gibbon believed that historians should be literary srtists, not researchers, and he disparaged manuscript work, utilizing only the best printed works he could find. Yet at the same time he encouraged others to engage in manuscript study and codification. In his writing Gibbon emphasized political and martial affairs, playing down social, cultural, and economic aspects—although they did receive mention. In this respect, he exhibited a narrow view of the content of history. Be that as it may, much of his work still stands as the best that has been written on such a monumental scale.

Some rationalist historians tended to stress emotionality rather than rationality, and thus they unknowingly provided a logical bridge to the romanticism of the next historiographic period.

7. Romantic Historiography

The Reformation had weakened religious faith, and the ideas of the Enlightenment, as reflected by the French Revolution, were considered by many to have been repudiated. The romantic reaction to Enlightenment rationality was an attempt to fill a religious and intellectual vacuum.

Romanticists believed in what is termed the cultural evolution of society, to which was added a solidarity of the human race concept. Emotion and personal feeling were stressed at the expense of the preceding rationality. The era witnessed a pronounced tendency to escape reality—to escape to the peace and beauty of nature, or to escape to far off places or far distant periods in history.

But the Enlightenment idea of natural rights was maintained and pushed to its extreme. Individuals became totally free; therefore, any artificial restriction placed upon them by society was wrong. The romantic historians demonstrated a high degree of sympathy toward social reform or political liberalism—any cause that might further individual freedom. Romantics were ardent nationalists and aided in the development of national literatures. They were equally ardent in their exposition of the "Great Man" theory[4] of history; after all, individuality received significant stress in their thinking. Running throughout romantic thought was a certain mystical quality. There is an unseen guiding spirit that is directing individuals in their cultural evolution.

One of the many great romantic school historians was Chateaubriand (1768–1848), a Frenchman who began his historical career rather conservatively. Following a religious conversion, Chateaubriand wrote his classic *Genius of Christianity,* in which he stressed the role of Christianity as the stimulus for the development of art and poetry and for human progress. Chateaubriand was very literary in his style and very much concerned with presenting detailed accounts of the physical setting of historical events. Pictorial descriptions were emphasized. Like other romantic historians, he had a penchant for hero worship and local color; and, imbued with nationalism and patriotism for his own country, he treated his nation's past with a certain sentimentality. This particular aspect of romantic writing was especially utilized by German romantics.

8. *Nationalist Historiography*

Seeds of nationalistic thought were found throughout romantic writings. Further impetus was given by the French Revolution and its influence on inculcating a nationalistic spirit in such countries as Germany and Spain. And no small influence came from the pen of Gobineau, who proclaimed a racist superiority in 1854. German thinkers in particular used his racist idea to support their nationalist school of history writing.

[4]The Great Man theory holds that history is the study of the biographies of the great leaders of given eras. Hence, the names "Age of Philip II," "Age of Louis XIV," and "Napoleonic Europe" are given to various historical periods.

The Englishman, Thomas Macaulay, is representative of the nationalist school. Like other nationalist historians, Macaulay wrote to glorify his nation's past. In this respect his famous work, *History of England,* was partisan, as were all other nationalistic histories. But Macaulay did display good analysis, and he made a brilliant contribution to historical literature, even if he did not make an equal contribution to historical method.

9. Critical-Scientific Historiography

In roughly the latter half of the nineteenth century, overlapping the romantic and nationalistic schools of historical interpretation, is found what might be regarded as either the critical or scientific school. Many of the adherents of this school may also exhibit some of the characteristics of either romantic or nationalistic writing.

Some progress in the direction of critical history writing had been made by the humanists, but this progress had been largely stifled by the events of the Reformation era. The Maurists, a group of Benedictine monks at Saint Maur in France, had developed the rudiments of critical historiography in the late seventeenth and early eighteenth centuries. The romantic conception of history as a broad evolving process gave further rise to the development of a critical historical method. Also instrumental was the growing nationalistic spirit, which led to a greater concern for proving or disproving, as the case may be, the accuracy of historical facts.

Probably the chief initiator of modern critical historiography was Barthold Niebuhr. His *Roman History* reflected considerable testing of the traditional documents and writings. But the outstanding figure in the school was Leopold von Ranke. He established the methodology for determining the authenticity of source materials, insisted on historical truth, and developed the notion of "inner criticism," i.e., studying the habits and attitudes of authors in order to better evaluate their interpretations. Von Ranke also insisted upon detached, objective assessment of the facts and put forth the idea that every age and every nation is dominated by some particular ideology that explains its behavior.

Francois Guizot (1787–1874) was the French equivalent of Von Ranke. He did considerable compiling and editing of documents on French history, and in this respect he was a nationalist. Guizot also organized the scientific movement in his country and established the French Historical Society as well. His *General History of European Civilization* was one of the first efforts at a European synthesis—Guizot was especially strong at synthesis. In this

category Guizot held an advantage over Von Ranke, who was en-
meshed in German history; yet in an overall evaluation Von Ranke
was probably the better scholar.

10. Twentieth-Century European Overview

Modern historical writing and research in Europe have both
gained and lost owing to twentieth-century chaos. Two bloody
wars, and the economic dislocation and suffering that were their
aftermath, hardly provided a contemplative atmosphere for historical inquiry. Yet these very wars nurtured a growing interest in historical study and caused historians to make a renewed attempt to
discover the reasons for their chaotic age.

Twentieth-century historical writing in France has been affect-
ed considerably by two major invasions from Germany and their
subsequent psychological effect. This provides some explanation
for the fact that many French historians have largely ignored the
last hundred years of their history. But there are some French historians who are seeking answers for the twentieth century and
have written some penetrating and objective studies of their nation.

Pierre Renouvin is one French historian who deals with the
modern era, specializing in diplomatic history. In his capacity as a
diplomatic historian, Renouvin has done considerable editing, e.g.,
French Diplomatic Documents, 1871-1914. He has made a concerted effort to be objective about the causes of World War I (a
subject about which Frenchmen are normally quite partisan), and
he does a good job, although at times an unconscious anti-German
attitude seeps through. Renouvin is strong on historical synthesis,
and this is especially important for a diplomatic historian. In various later works he has covered diplomatic history through 1945.

The major concern of many modern French historians is the
French Revolution. Another major concern is social and economic history, and yet another is the compilation of the monumental
historical series, in which numerous authors write sections on their
own special periods and topics. In this respect, Ernest Lavisse is an
important individual. Under his direction a nine volume *History of
France From its Origins to the Revolution,* a ten volume *History
of Contemporary France From the Revolution to the Peace of
1919,* and, his most important, *Peoples and Civilizations* have been
written. However, these works have not been translated into English. Other joint projects included *General History* and *Evolution
of Humanity.*

In England, too, the modern trend is to the multi-volumed historical series. The *Cambridge Modern History* (13 volumes), the

Cambridge Medieval History (8 volumes), and the *Cambridge Ancient History* (12 volumes) reflect this trand. Another such work is the *Oxford History of England.*

Prior to World War I, English historians were concerned with studies of the common man and studies on the British imperial and diplomatic systems. The first consideration reflected the reform spirit then prevalent; the second reflected the peculiar nature of the Commonwealth system. The concern for diplomatic studies has continued throughout the twentieth century, with major impetus having been provided by the release of numerous "secret" documents during the inter-war period. English historians are engaged in a continual revision of their past studies and have exhibited a growing interest in economic history.

A representative modern English historian dealing with the contemporary era is Charles Webster. His concern is mainly with the wars and diplomacy of the nineteenth and twentieth centuries. And he is quite optimistic about the future fate of humankind. Webster attended the Versailles peace conference at the close of World War I as an English officer and an expert on the Congress of Vienna. As such he gained a detailed, first-hand knowledge of what was transpiring there. During the following decades Webster devoted his energies to prodding various governments to make their diplomatic records available to historians. He was a proponent of the League of Nations and wrote on it. Later on his active role in the formation of the United Nations led to knighthood. Currently, a history of the RAF during World War II is being prepared under the auspices of the English Government. Mention should also be made of Arnold Toynbee.[5] His challenge and response interpretation of history has stimulated many historians to think more meaningfully about the structure and purpose of their discipline.

Revisionism in England has given rise to a quantitative approach to historical interpretation. It is reflected by Sir Lewis Namier, whose *England in the Age of the American Revolution* (1930) utilizes a behavioral approach in attempting to explain why Parliament acted as it did. In effect, Namier and the historians who accept his position attempt to make use of the tools of the behavioral school of political science by directly applying the technique to appropriate aspects of historical inquiry.[6]

A very difficult nation to summarize briefly is modern Germany. The history writing of Germany varies, but a major portion of the twentieth century is characterized by writing that reflects

[5]*Supra,* Chapter 3.
[6]*Supra,* pp. 65-66.

intense nationalism, undemocratic spirit, and control by an elite group. During the world wars, German history writing took the form of propaganda (as is the case with most warring nations). After World War I the primary concern was exoneration of war guilt, and in this task, German historians were aided by the release of many documents by the Weimar government. In the post-World War II era, German historians are attempting to cope with a most difficult situation: the Third Reich and reunification. Yet there is a different theme in modern German historiography. A few writers emphasize human purpose in their philosophy of history; so there is a strand of idealism and optimism running through the historiography of a disillusioned nation. Twentieth-century Germany has contributed Friederich Meinecke, who has performed creditable service in strengthening the Von Ranke approach to historical study. Meinecke is widely regarded as the most able historian produced by Germany since Von Ranke. His approach is intellectual, a playing down of institutional and traditional political history and a studying of political ideas to uncover the dominant concepts of each epoch. Considerable attention has been given by Meinecke to the concepts of liberalism and nationalism.

In Russian historiography the major pre-revolutionary emphasis was on economic matters, and this quickly turned into economic determinism. The revolutionary period was dominated by the Marxian philosophy of history. Moving away from the revolution, under Soviet Party direction, emphasis was placed more upon historical fact and less on abstract ideas. But the purpose of contemporary Soviet writers is to instill in the Russian people a sense of nationalism and unity in the Soviet regime.

During World War II the tendency in the Soviet Union was toward wartime propaganda, but this did not affect Russian historiography as much as that of other warring nations, for the simple fact that propaganda had been very much a part of Russian history writing for some time. Politics continue to dominate Russian history today. Those historians who have left Russia have made significant contributions to Russian historiography.

Balkan historiography reflects the changes in Balkan countries in the twentieth century. Up to the end of World War I the dominant trend in writing consisted of an emphasis on independence—hence, nationalistic history. During the inter-war period historians sought to justify independence to the rest of the world by tracing the origins of their respective nations. World War II brought Communist control for the Balkans, and history writing, as in Russia, was used for political purposes.

Among Austrian historians the idea of nationalism was quite strong, first in the treatment of the Dual Monarchy, and then in the "Middle Europe" idea. A more radical nationalism came with Nazi rule. After World War II Austrian historians returned to solid scholarship. Austrian medievalists in particular have done a creditable job.

Hungarian historiography was dominated by the independence theme up to World War I; this was at the expense of Austria. During the inter-war period the main theme concerned a penetrating search for the spiritual motivation that was reputed to be at the base of historical fact. Since coming under Communist control, Hungarian historiography has been dominated by political considerations.

In modern Belgian historiography there is an enormous effort to collect archival materials in numerous monographic studies. These are published in the many Belgian professional journals. Belgium's greatest modern historian, Henri Pirenne (d. 1935), is best known for his studies in medieval economic history, but his main concern was with the effect of economic factors on the shaping of society. Imbued in the Von Ranke approach to historical study, Pirenne's interest covered the breadth of Western civilization; he felt the need for synthesis, although he admitted that any synthesizing was necessarily in a constant state of flux. His voluminous writings covered subjects extending well into the 1900's.

Italy has contributed little to twentieth century historiography. The highly influential Benedetto Croce held that history is an art form. Hence history is subject to intuition and the creative impulse and is rather nonscientific. World War I brought about a revival of more solid scholarship as Italians sought to discover the reasons for the preceding state of affairs. But fascism from the 1920's forward destroyed objectivity, as is witnessed by the propaganda type of history written. Most good Italian historians today concern themselves with the ancient past.

Spanish history writing reflects an interest in joint projects. History writing was generally liberal for the first three decades of the century, but this characteristic waned under fascist rule. Spanish historians tend to concentrate on the pre-nineteenth century era, particularly on Spain's "Golden Century."

What applies for Spain also applies for Portugal, except for the development pertaining to fascism. Portugal likewise concentrates on its age of greatness. Joint projects are quite popular.

To obtain a detailed knowledge of modern trends in European historiography, one must consult monographic articles on the subject in the various professional journals. The subject of historiography is exceedingly complex, but no historian is able to function well without a knowledge of it.

There is currently a historical school known as historical relativism. Adherents believe that historians accept as historically true only what their climate of opinion allows them to accept, and that emotional factors create shifts in what is accepted as true from time to time. Advocates of historical relativity further believe that the past is so complex that it can never be known completely, that the only reason for even bothering with it is to obtain some utilitarian value for the present and future. Some historians are guilty of this creation of a changing past, especially those who have held government positions. They occasionally become, in effect, "court historians," and reflect the official government position as it is then being championed. Such views are hardly within the Von Ranke framework of scientific, historical inquiry. The presence of various schools of historical thought necessitates a knowledge of historiography on the part of students of history if they are to accurately evaluate the authenticity of historical writings.

Questions for Discussion

1.   Illustrate the ways in which later schools of European historiography developed Thucydides' notion of the utility of history.

2.   Discuss why historical interpretation under the influence of the early Christian Church resulted in rather poor historical writing.

3.   Characterize and evaluate major historiographical trends in the major nations of modern Europe.

4.   Discuss the effects of the Renaissance and Reformation on the development of historical writing.

5.   Compare and contrast the various periods of European historiography. Which period do you feel yielded the greatest contribution toward the development of solid historical scholarship and why?

Two New Trends in American Historiography

7

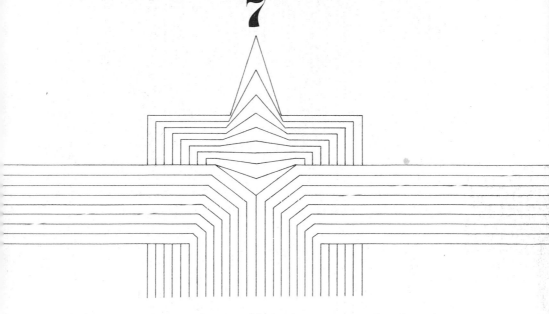

It is a common practice to add portions to a previously published work to bring it more nearly up to date; the present work is no exception. Much has happened in the field of American historiography since 1967 when this book was first published. Two trends in particular—the developing historiographies of women and blacks—are entitled to far greater attention than a summary inclusion in Chapter 5 would allow.

American historical writing, until very recently, has been the province of white males; and they have by and large written about a white male-oriented society. The cultural milieu within which American historians have traditionally operated has precluded them from giving more than cursory attention to the roles, contributions, and achievements of two very large groups of people in American society: women (comprising approximately 51 percent of the population) and blacks (comprising approximately 11 percent of the population).

It is not the case, of course, that American women and blacks have failed to produce any historical works of their own. But the writings of blacks were read mainly by blacks, and the writings of women were read primarily by women; the writings of both groups were either scorned or ignored by most white male historians. Thus, except for references to the women's suffrage movement or to the institution of slavery or to individual women and blacks who simply could not be ignored (e.g., Margaret Fuller and George Washington Carver), the works of women and blacks have generally been overlooked.

The present chapter proposes to briefly survey the nascent historiographies of these two neglected groups of Americans, historiographies made possible largely through the efforts of the civil rights and women's movements of the post-World War II decades. After years of abuse, attention is at last being shifted to the large gaps that exist in the historiographies of women and blacks, historiographies that are quite sparse prior to the twentieth century.

The fact that attention is now being directed to hitherto forgotten groups of Americans illustrates the idea of history as a dynamic process of reinterpreting the past in light of the contemporary cultural milieu and the availability of new evidence. This new chapter highlights in a very substantive, practical way the problems encountered in the study of history which we discussed in theoretical terms in Chapter 2.

1. Women's Historiography

Women's historiography, of course, is not the same as women's literature. Historiography, as we discussed at the beginning of Chapter 5, is concerned with what historians write about history— their methodology, interpretations, values, evidence, validity of conclusions, and so forth. Women's literature, on the other hand, is an all-encompassing subject, embracing all aspects of women. Women's historiography is just one of many topics subsumed under the general heading of women's literature. Furthermore, the literature of any movement, especially when its writers sincerely and wholeheartedly adhere to the goals and aspirations of the movement, is rarely objective. Propaganda, no matter how worthy the motives of its propagators, is not history and, therefore, is not within the scope of women's historiography.

Except for the suffragists and other prominent female reformers, little has been written in American history about women, their lives, contributions, and achievements until the contemporary era. While it is true that a number of prominent female reformers have been discussed in most history textbooks, these women are hardly representative. It is almost a truism that any reform leader is at least somewhat out of the mainstream of society; for centuries a woman who did anything other than tend to her family and household chores was even more atypical. If it is true that the "common man" has been neglected in historical writing until the modern era, what must be the case of the "common woman"?

Nineteenth century women's history frequently consisted of observations by women on their condition in society. Oftentimes these observations took the form of personal memoirs and tended to be didactic and moralistic. These personal observations, of course, are not ideal historical writings; but they can, to a certain degree, be classified as primary works. One of the better historical works was Lucy Maynard Salmon's *Domestic Service* published in 1897. Her book dealt with what happened to the women left behind when large numbers of men moved westward to settle the frontier. Another notable book on another aspect of the same subject was William Fowler's *Woman on the American Frontier* published in 1878.

Nineteenth-century women's writing also took the form of biographical compilations, as some women sought to preserve the achievements of members of their sex for posterity. A very comprehensive listing of nineteenth-century women of achievement written in 1882 was Phoebe A. Hanaford's *Daughters of America: Or Women of the Century;* it remains an important source work for women's studies.

Unfortunately, no general history of American women was written during the nineteenth century. Some monographic studies (most of them concerned with the suffragist movement), numerous memoirs and observations, and other writings not within the realm of historiographical inquiry comprise the women's oeuvre of the century. Thus, prior to the twentieth century the possibilities of research in the area of women's historiography are slim indeed.

Unique in her prominence at the opening of the twentieth century and well qualified as an historian, Mary Ritter Beard coauthored historical works with her husband, Charles Austin Beard; she produced notable historical works dealing with women on her own during and after the World War I era. Her *Woman As Force in History* was recently republished in 1971.

A hallmark event in women's studies was the publication of Ernest Groves's *The American Woman: The Feminine Side of a Masculine Civilization* in 1924. In this work Groves chided historians for not giving women a proper place in American history.

Despite the awakened interest in women's studies in the twentieth century, a general women's history remains to be written. It should be pointed out, however, that the monographic studies that have been written are different from most earlier works on women;

recent monographic studies do constitute authentic professional
history and they are well researched. Perhaps the main reason why
a general women's history has not been written is that the source
materials for such an undertaking have yet to be collected, cata-
logued, and synthesized. As a result, modern women's historiography is concerned primarily with the compilation of source materials—collections of earlier misplaced or forgotten works, biographical data, memoirs, and tracts.

A very recent (1972) and highly significant compilation of
source materials edited by Annette K. Baxter and Leon Stein is
American Women: Images and Realities, a forty-four-volume collection of writings about women by women throughout American
history. Most of the selections contained in this collection appear
to be useful source materials for the writing of a women's history.
Another compilation is Jerome S. Ozer's *Women's Rights and
Liberation* published in 1969, a five-book collection of the writings of leading American women of the nineteenth century, e.g.,
Susan B. Anthony, Julia Ward Howe, and Elizabeth Cady Stanton.
This collection consists of biographies, diaries, speeches, and minutes of meetings. Yet another notable source collection is the
Arthur and Elizabeth Schlesinger Library on the History of Women
in America at Radcliffe College. This library contains over 12,000
volumes, 200 major collections, and 31 archival collections.

As a result of this type of compiling and synthesizing, the pros-
pects for improved women's history within the next decade are
great. If improved women's history does come about (and the
trend is more than discernible), women's historiography will solid-
ify because of the widespread availability of secondary works.

Some of these secondary works have already been written.
Sheila Rowbotham, a British historian, wrote *Women, Resistance
and Revolution: A History of Women and Revolution in the Modern World* in 1973 which traces the history of both European and
American women from the late Renaissance to the early twentieth
century. Of even broader scope is Vern L. Bullough's 1973 study,
The Subordinate Sex: A History of Attitudes Toward Women,
which marks the first cross-cultural, historical study of attitudes
toward women from ancient times to the present day. Also in the
contemporary era is Eleanor Flexner's *Century of Struggle: The
Women's Rights Movement in the United States* first published in
1959. This work makes notable contributions to historiography in
general and to women's historiography in particular. The serious
student of women's historiography should not overlook the scholarly work edited by Miriam Schneir, *Feminism: The Essential Historical Writings,* published in 1971.

Male historians have also become progressively more involved in women's historiography. Arthur Schlesinger's *New Viewpoints in American History*, published in 1922, included a chapter entitled "The Role of Women in American History." Currently, Carl N. Degler is working on a book exploring the role of women in American society. Thus, it appears that the spirit of the times and the growing availability of source materials are creating a dramatic change in American historical writings.

The concern for a women's historiography has naturally produced some outstanding female historians in the contemporary era. Besides those mentioned previously, two very prominent historians are Gerda Lerner and Ann Firor Scott. The Western Group of the American Historical Association has established a women's branch; and numerous foundations, educational institutions, and publishing houses are making a concerted effort to produce a viable women's history.

2.   Black Historiography

Black historiography has many parallels with women's historiography. Both groups have, to a large extent, been robbed of their respective histories. Historians have failed to study the black past carefully; but it is important to note that, unlike women's history, a definite black history exists prior to the twentieth century.

Black history is simply the history of blacks in America and other parts of the world. Black history arose because it was obvious to blacks that they were systematically being excluded from historical writings, because there was a need to combat racial prejudice and stereotypes, and because blacks wanted to instill a sense of pride in their own racial heritage by providing models for the emulation of young blacks. In this last respect early black history was similar to early women's history in that both were largely devoted to the writing of biographies of prominent individuals.

Among nineteenth-century black history writers, William Cooper Nell wrote factually on early black military contributions in his *Colored Patriots of the American Revolution*, published in 1855. George Washington Williams wrote the first general black history in 1883, *A History of the Negro Race in America from 1619 to 1880*. William's scholarship was noteworthy; but, like most nineteenth-century writers, his interpretations were quite moralistic. Booker T. Washington's *The Story of the Negro: The Rise of the Race from Slavery* was well received and offered some consideration of social history, but the book was poorly documented and otherwise reiterated what George Washington Williams had already written. But it should be pointed out that Washington's book did serve the useful purpose of popularizing black history.

Generally speaking, the theme of racial uplift was the single most prominent characteristic of nineteenth-century black historians. Nineteenth-century history was written to justify emancipation and equality by pointing to black achievements. However, most nineteenth-century black history writers were not professionally trained historians. The essential merit of writers such as George Washington Williams, Booker T. Washington, Prince Saunders, Paul Cuffee, and others was that they reflected the beginning of an awakening interest in the black past.

A prominent black scholar at the turn of the century was W. E. B. Du Bois, the first of his race to earn a Ph.D. from Harvard. Trained in the German scientific school (Du Bois studied at Berlin), his geographical separation from America enabled him to develop a unique perspective on the American race issue. His *The Suppression of the African-Slave Trade to the United States of America*, published in 1896, was well written and paved the way for black historical studies. His *The Philadelphia Negro: A Social Study*, published in 1899, was one of the first sociological studies written in America. Following years of teaching and involvement in the NAACP, Du Bois toured Russia and turned Marxist. Thus his *Black Reconstruction in America, 1860–1880* was written from the perspective of an economic determinist, while later works depicted blacks as the impoverished masses being exploited on a worldwide scale by the capitalist class. The writings of Du Bois comprise a distinct contribution to black historiography in particular and to American historiography in general.

The opening decades of the twentieth century bore witness to several changes in black history. Blacks were beginning to achieve hitherto unknown success in the educational, financial, and intellectual realms. During the World War I era, this success was coupled with the beginning of a large movement of blacks from the rural South to Northern urban centers. Racial pressures and concentrated numbers contributed to the development of new attitudes.

Whereas earlier black writers had attempted to *justify* equality, twentieth-century writers *assumed* equality and reacted strongly to the doctrine of white supremacy that was explicitly or implicitly being taught in the public schools. New black writers were university trained. New historical writings were much more scholarly than earlier works, but the new writings were still propagandistic. Whereas equality had been the stated objective of earlier writers, the new black historians saw freedom as their objective.

Highly prominent among black historians throughout the first half of the twentieth century was Carter G. Woodson, the reputed "father of black history." He believed that racial prejudice in America was the direct result of miseducation. He posited three basic purposes for the writing of black history: to demonstrate that blacks had been ignored in historical writings; to make blacks aware of the achievements of other blacks in order to motivate them; and to prove to whites that blacks had made solid contributions to the human race, thereby (hopefully) creating white respect. These stated purposes of black history, as proposed by Woodson, were and largely still are the central characteristics of black historical writings. History was envisioned as a weapon which could be used to fight racial inequality, especially after European archaeologists and anthropologists made discoveries proving the existence of advanced African civilizations.

It was Carter Woodson who developed the recognition of black history as a distinct field of scholarly inquiry. In 1915 he founded the Association for the Study of Negro Life and History to encourage scholars to engage in the intensive study of the black past. In 1916 he founded the famous *Journal of Negro History* and in 1926 the *Negro History Weekly*. A recurring theme in Woodson's voluminous writings, best known of which was his 1922 college text, *The Negro in Our History*, was that racial prejudice was the result of a misguided educational process. Blacks, he believed, had to be educated in order to appreciate themselves. In order to bring out books on black life and culture, he founded and became president of Associated Publishers while a dean at West Virginia State College, thereby providing publication opportunities for black writers. Although Woodson's writing style possessed shortcomings, he is responsible for making black history viable both on scholarly and popular levels and for making possible the full development of black historiography. American women, unfortunately, possessed no such counterpart in their historiographic development.

Woodson almost singlehandedly created a desire for black studies. As a consequence of his work and efforts, black historians such as Merl Eppse, Charles Wesley, and Monroe Work labored to establish black studies programs. Work also wrote the *Bibliography of the Negro in Africa and America* in 1928, a work that is still very useful and informative.

Modern black historiography since World War II is characterized by scholarly documentation, only a passing concern for refuting racist charges, little use of propagandizing and moralizing, and an attempt to avoid an exclusively black theme. Black history has become a specialty area in American history just like other specialty areas. Some modern black historians, of course, have specialized in nonblack areas. Clinton Knox and Eric Williams, for example, have specialized in European history; and Rayford Logan is a well-known scholar concentrating on diplomatic history.

Nevertheless, a large number of modern black historians are concerned primarily with recording the history of American blacks. A representative sampling of those working in this area consists of Lorenzo Greene, Benjamin Quarles, Leslie Fishel, Edgar Toppin, William Strickland, and Earl Thorpe. A good current black history text, *From Slavery to Freedom: A History of American Negroes,* was written by John Hope Franklin in 1967.

Two white historians who have written significantly about black history in recent years are Kenneth Stampp and Carl N. Degler. Stampp's *The Peculiar Institution* (1956) and Degler's *Neither Black Nor White: Slavery and Race Relations in Brazil and the U.S.* (1971) are two books that have helped shape current thinking about the crucial issue of black slavery.

Mention should also be made of modern black history source works. Maxwell Whiteman edited the *Afro-American History Series* in 1972, a ten-volume collection of pamphlets and other short works written by blacks of every social position throughout American history. Guy T. Westmoreland's *An Annotated Guide to Basic Reference Books on the Black American Experience* was published in 1974. A good basic bibliography on black authors is to be found in Benjamin Quarles's 1964 *The Negro in the Making of America.* In addition, black historians are beginning to analyze their own historiography. Dwight W. Hoover's *Understanding Negro History* (1968) and Earl Thorpe's *Black Historians: A Critique of Black Historians* (1971) are both very valuable works on black historiography.

Bibliography

Appendix A

A bibliography may have several purposes. One purpose is to inform the reader of those works that the author has consulted in writing his own work. The present bibliography is compiled only partially with this purpose in mind. A second purpose of a bibliography is to present to the reader an exhaustive list of works written on a particular subject. Again, this is not the purpose of the present bibliography. This book is designed to serve as an introductory guide to the discipline of history. Only in the listing of guides to published materials has a degree of thoroughness been attempted. And even here, in consideration of the intended reader, foreign language works and bibliographies, a number of the more obscure and specialized bibliographies, and bibliographies in the area of guides to manuscript materials and collections have been excluded.

A third purpose of a bibliography is to develop for the benefit of the reader a selected sampling of some of the works available on a given subject for further, more detailed reading. This is the only claim made for the present bibliography. If the reader should happen to desire a more complete list of works, the bibliographical guides listed in this bibliography, as well as in many of the works themselves, should provide whatever information he or she desires.

For the convenience of the reader the following bibliographical entries are grouped within broad categories of interest.

1. Works on Methodology

Barzun, Jacques, and Graff, Henry. *The Modern Researcher*. New York: Harcourt, Brace & World, 1957.

Becker, Carl. *Everyman His Own Historian*. New York: Appleton-Century-Crofts, 1935.

Berkhofer, Robert F. *A Behavioral Approach to Historical Analysis*. New York: Macmillan, 1969.

Bloch, M. *The Historian's Craft*. New York: Alfred A. Knopf, Inc., 1953.

Fling, Fred M. *The Writing of History: An Introduction to Historical Method*. New Haven: The Yale University Press, 1920.

Garraghan, Gilbert J. *A Guide to Historical Method*. Edited by Jean Delanglez. New York: Fordham University Press, 1956.
    A very scholarly, advanced guide.

Geyl, Pieter. *The Use and Abuse of History*. New Haven: The Yale University Press, 1955.

Gilbert, Felix, and Graubard, Stephen. *Historical Studies Today*. New York: Norton, 1972.

Gray, Wood, *et al. Historian's Handbook*. 2nd ed. Boston: Houghton Mifflin Company, 1964.
Contains good basic bibliographies for all fields of historical inquiry.

Gustavson, Carl. *A Preface to History*. New York: McGraw-Hill, 1955.
An extremely enlightening work—quite suitable for the beginning student.

Hexter, J. H. *Reappraisals in History*. New York: Harper & Row, Publishers, 1961.

Hockett, Homer C. *The Critical Method in Historical Research and Writing*. New York: The Macmillan Company, 1955.

Hoover, Dwight W. (ed.). *Understanding Negro History*. New York: Quadrangle Books, 1968.

Kent, Sherman. *Writing History*, 2nd ed. New York: Appleton-Century-Crofts, 1967.

Lucey, William L. *History: Methods and Interpretation*. Chicago: Loyola University Press, 1958.

Nevins, Allan. *Gateway to History*. rev. ed. Boston: D. C. Heath, 1962.

Renier, Gustaf. *History: Its Purpose and Method*. Boston: The Beacon Press, 1950.

Saveth, Edward N. (ed.). *American History and the Social Sciences*. Glencoe, Illinois: The Free Press, 1964.
Describes the natural integration of the various disciplines.

Schafer, Boyd C., *et al. Historical Studies in the West*. New York: Appleton-Century-Crofts, 1968.

2. Works on Philosophy of History

Barraclough, Geoffrey. *History in a Changing World*. Oxford: The Blackwell Press, 1955.

Butterfield, Herbert. *Man on His Past*. Boston: Beacon Press, 1960.

Cairns, Grace E. *Philosophies of History: Meeting of East and West in Cycle-Pattern Theories of History*. New York: Philosophical Library, 1962.

Carr, Edward H. *What Is History?* New York: Alfred A. Knopf, Inc., 1962.

Cassirer, Ernst. *The Logic of the Humanities*. New Haven: Yale University Press, 1961.

Childe, V. Gordon. *What Is History?* New York: H. Schuman Company, 1953.

Collingwood, R. G. *The Idea of History*. Oxford: The Clarendon Press, 1946.

D'Arcy, Martin C. *The Sense of History*. London: Faber and Faber, 1959.

Dray, William H. *Philosophy of History*. Englewood Cliffs, New Jersey: Prentice-Hall, Inc., 1964.
A good survey of the various approaches.

Eliade, M. *Myth of the Eternal Reunion: Cosmos and History*. Princeton: Princeton University Press, 1971.

Gardiner, Patrick (ed.). *Theories of History*. Glencoe, Illinois: The Free Press, 1959.

Geyl, Pieter. *Debates with Historians*. Cleveland: Meridian Books.

Gottschalk, Louis. *Understanding History*. New York: Alfred A. Knopf, Inc., 1950.

Halvdan, Koht. *Driving Forces in History*. Cambridge: Harvard University Press, 1964.

Klibansky, Raymond, and Paton, H. J. (eds.). *Philosophy and History: Essays Presented to Ernst Cassirer.* New York: Harper & Row, Publishers, 1963.

Kubler, George A. *Shape of Time: Remarks on the History of Things.* New Haven: Yale University Press, 1962.

Lowith, Karl. *Meaning in History: The Theological Implications of the Philosophy of History.* Chicago: The University of Chicago Press, 1959.

Malin, J. C. *On the Nature of History: Essays About History and Dissidence.* Lawrence, Kansas: By the Author, 1954.

Muller, Herbert J. *The Uses of the Past: Profiles of Former Societies.* New York: Oxford University Press, 1952.

Ortega y Gasset, Jose. *History as a System: And Other Essays Toward a Philosophy of History.* New York: W. W. Norton & Company, Inc., 1961.

Pieper, Josef. *The End of Time: A Meditation on the Philosophy of History.* Translated by M. Bulloch. New York: Pantheon Books, 1954.

Rowse, A. L. *The Use of History.* New York: The Macmillan Company, 1947.

Russell, Bertrand. *Understanding History and Other Essays.* New York: Philosophical Library, 1957.

Stern, Fritz. *The Varieties of History.* Cleveland: World Publishing Company, 1956. Also available in paperback, Cleveland: Meridian Books, 1956.

Strayer, Joseph R. (ed.). *The Interpretation of History.* Princeton: Princeton University Press, 1943. Reprinted New York: Peter Smith, 1950.

Teggart, Frederick J. *Theory and Processes in History.* Berkeley: University of California Press, 1941.

Toulmin, Stephen, and Goodfield, June. *The Discovery of Time.* New York: Harper & Row, 1965.

3. Guide to Bibliographies

The bibliographies contained in this section pertain only to works written in the English language. Further information may be found in Nevins' *Gateway to History.* Listed below are basic bibliographies for all geographical divisions of history, including foreign language works, excellent bibliographies contained in the Langer series, the Bibliography of British History series, and the older Cambridge historical series.

American Catalogue of Books, 1876-1910. New York: Publishers Weekly, 1881-1911.

Annual American Catalogue, 1886-1910. New York: Publishers Weekly, 1887-1911.

Beers, Henry P. *Bibliographies in American History.* rev. ed. New York: The H. W. Wilson Company, 1942.
   The work contains over 11,000 indexed entries.

Bemis, Samuel F., and Griffin, Grace G. *Guide to the Diplomatic History of the United States, 1775-1921.* Washington: Government Printing Office, 1935.

Besterman, Theodore. *A World Bibliography of Bibliographies.* 3rd ed. Geneva: Societas Bibliographica, 1955-1956.

Billington, Ray A. *Westward Expansion.* 2nd ed. New York: The Macmillan Company, 1960.
   Although this is a textbook, its bibliography warrants its inclusion here.

Cambridge Ancient History, The. 12 vols. New York: The Macmillan Company, 1923-1939.
   The Cambridge series possesses extensive chapter bibliographies.

Cambridge Bibliography of English Literature, 600–1900. 5 vols. New York: The Macmillan Company, 1941–1957.

Cambridge Medieval History, The. 8 vols. New York: The Macmillan Company, 1911–1936.

Cambridge Modern History, The. 13 vols. New York: The Macmillan Company, 1902–1926.

Catalogue of Printed Books in the Library of the British Museum. 95 vols. London: William Clowes and Sons, Ltd., 1881–1900. Supplement, 1900–1905. 15 vols.
> *General Catalogue of Printed Books.* 51 vols. 1934–1956, carries the series forward.

Channing, Edward; Hart, Albert; and Turner, Frederick J. *Guide to the Study and Reading of American History.* rev. ed. Boston: Ginn and Company, 1912.
> The work covers what had been written up to 1910 and is consequently not up to date, but it has been superseded by the *Harvard Guide* listed below.

Clark, G. N. (ed.). *The Oxford History of England.* 14 vols. New York: Oxford University Press, 1934–1961.

Cumulative Book Index. New York: The H. W. Wilson Company, 1898–.
> Lists everything written in the English language and published anywhere in the world.

Cuthbertson, Stuart, and Ewers, John. *A Preliminary Bibliography of the American Fur Trade.* St. Louis: Jefferson National Expansion Memorial, 1938.
> The work is of much broader scope than the title would indicate.

English Catalogue of Books, 1801–. London: Publisher's Circular, 1837–.
> Now published quarterly.

Evans, Charles. *American Bibliography, 1639–1820.* 13 vols. Chicago: The Blakely Press, 1903–1934.
> The work is indexed.

Gohdes, Clarence L. *Bibliographical Guide to the Study of the Literature of the U.S.A.* Durham, North Carolina: Duke University Press, 1959.

Griffin, A. P., comp. *Bibliography of American Historical Societies.* Washington: Government Printing Office, 1907.
> Originally the Report of the American Historical Association for 1905.

Handlin, Oscar, *et al. Harvard Guide to American History.* Cambridge: Harvard University Press, 1954.
> Covers the period up to 1950.

Howe, George F. *Guide to Historical Literature.* New York: The Macmillan Company, 1961.

International Index: A Guide to Periodical Literature in the Social Sciences and Humanities. New York: The H. W. Wilson Company, 1907–.
> Kept up to date with quarterly supplements.

Jones, Howard M. *Guide to American Literature and Its Backgrounds Since 1890.* 2nd rev. ed. Cambridge: Harvard University Press, 1959.

Kelly, James. *American Catalogue of Books Published in the United States from January 1861 to January 1871.* 2 vols. New York: Wiley Company, 1866–1871.

Krichmar, Albert. *The Women's Rights Movement in the United States 1848–1970: A Bibliography and Sourcebook.* Metuchen, New Jersey: The Scarecrow Press, Inc., 1972.

Langer, William L. (ed.). *The Rise of Modern Europe.* 20 vols. New York: Harper & Row, 1934—.

Matthews, William, and Pearce, Roy. *American Diaries: An Annotated Bibliography of American Diaries Written Prior to the Year 1861.* Berkeley: University of California Press, 1945.

National Union Catalogue. 28 vols. Ann Arbor: Edwards Company, 1958. Covers the years 1953-1957 and includes works that are not listed in the Library of Congress publications noted below.

New York Times Index. New York Times, 1913.

Paetow, Louis J. *A Guide to the Study of Medieval History.* rev. ed. New York: F. S. Crofts and Company, 1931.

Poole's Index to Periodical Literature, 1802-1881. rev. ed. 2 vols. Boston: Houghton Mifflin Company, 1891. Supplements carry the work to 1906.

Poulton, Helen J. *The Historian's Handbook: A Descriptive Guide to Reference Works.* Norman: University of Oklahoma Press, 1972.

Ragatz, Lowell. *A Bibliography for the Study of European History, 1815-1939.* Ann Arbor: Edwards Brothers, 1942.

Reader's Guide to Periodical Literature. New York: The H. W. Wilson Company, 1900—. Issued monthly and bound annually.

Reed, Conoyers. *Bibliography of British History: Tudor Period, 1485-1603.* 2nd ed. Oxford: Clarendon Press, 1959. Other volumes are in process to bring the series forward by historical period.

Roorback, Orville. *Bibliotheca Americana, 1820-1861.* 4 vols. New York: A. O. Roorback, 1852-1861. Arranged in alphabetical order.

Sabine, Joseph, *et al. Dictionary of Books Relating to America from Its Discovery to the Present Time.* 29 vols. New York: J. Sabine, 1868-1936. Lists more than 106,000 items.

Thorpe, Earle. *Black Historians: A Critique.* New York: William Morrow and Company, Inc., 1971. Contains a good bibliography.

United States Catalogue, 1900—. Marion E. Potter, *et al.,* eds. New York: The H. W. Wilson Company, 1900—.

United States, Library of Congress. *Catalogue of Books Represented By Library of Congress Printed Cards.* 167 vols. Ann Arbor: Edwards Company, 1942-1946. Covers the period 1898-1942. *Supplement.* 42 vols. Ann Arbor: Edwards Company, 1948. Covers the years 1942-1947.

United States, Library of Congress. *The Library of Congress Author Catalogue.* 24 vols. Ann Arbor: Edwards Company, 1953. Covers the years 1948-1952.

United States, Library of Congress. *The Library of Congress, Books: Subjects.* 20 vols. Ann Arbor: Edwards Company, 1955. Covers the period 1950-1954. Additional coverage by a different publishing house as follows: 22 vols. Patterson, New Jersey: Pageant Books, 1961. Covers the years 1955-1959.

Westmoreland, Guy T. *An Annotated Guide to Basic Reference Books on the Black American Experience.* Washington, D.C.: Scholarly Reasources, Inc., 1974.

Wheeler, Helen. *Womanhood Media: Current Resources About Women*.
    Metuchen, New Jersey: The Scarecrow Press, Inc., 1972.
Winchell, Constance (ed.). *Guide to Reference Books*. 7th ed. Chicago:
    American Library Association, 1951.
    First edition appeared in 1930.

4. Writings on American History

Griffin, Grace G. *Writings on American History, 1906-1940*. Volumes for
    different years are published by different companies as follows:
    1906-1908—3 vols. New York: The Macmillan Company, 1908-1910.
    1909-1911—3 vols. Washington: Government Printing Office, 1911-1913.
    1912-1917—6 vols. New Haven: Yale University Press, 1914-1919.
    1918-1940—21 vols. American Historical Association, *Annual Report*.
McLaughlin, Andrew C., *et al. Writings on American History, 1903*. Washing-
    ton: The Carnegie Institution, 1905.
Masterson, James E. *Writings on American History, 1948–*. American Histor-
    ical Association, *Annual Report*.
Richardson, Ernest, and Anson, Ely. *Writings on American History, 1902*.
    Princeton: Library Bookstore, 1904.
    Despite the work accomplished by individuals and under the sanction of
    the American Historical Association, there still remain gaps for 1904–
    1905 and 1941-1947.

5. Basic Reference Works

Barnhart, Clarence L., and Halsey, William D. (eds.). *The New Century
    Cyclopedia of Names*. 3 vols. New York: Appleton-Century-Crofts, Inc.,
    1954.
Book Review Digest, 1905–. New York: The H. W. Wilson Company, 1905–.
Langer, William, and Gatzke, Hans (eds.). *An Encyclopedia of World History,
    Ancient, Medieval, and Modern, Chronologically Arranged*. rev. ed. Bos-
    ton: Houghton Mifflin Company, 1956.
Morris, Richard B. (ed.). *Encyclopedia of American History*. New York:
    Harper & Brothers, Publishers, 1953.
Palmer, Robert, *et al. Atlas of World History*. Chicago: Rand McNally &
    Company, 1957.
Pauk, Walter. *How to Study in College*. Boston: Houghton Mifflin Company,
    1962.
Paullin, Charles O. *Atlas of the Historical Geography of the United States*.
    New York: American Geographical Society, 1932
Pugh, Griffith T. *Guide to Research Writing*. 2nd ed. Boston: Houghton
    Mifflin Company, 1963.
    Strong on bibliographical entry and footnote citation.
Roeder, William S. *Dictionary of European History*. New York: Philosophical
    Library, 1954.
Spiller, Robert, *et al. Literary History of the United States*. New York: The
    Macmillan Company, 1948.
Turabian, Kate L. *A Manual for Writers of Term Papers, Theses, and Disserta-
    tions*. rev. ed. Chicago: The University of Chicago Press, 1955.
United States, Library of Congress. *A Guide to the Study of the United States
    of America*. Washington: Government Printing Office, 1960.
United States, Library of Congress, General Reference and Bibliography Divi-

sion. *List of National Archives Microfilms.* Washington: Government
Printing Office, 1961
Constantly being revised—covers period from 1940 forward.

6. Biographical Guides

Biography Index. New York: The H. W. Wilson Company, 1946—.
Supplemented monthly by *Current Biography.* New York: The H. W.
Wilson Company.
Cattell, Jacques (ed.). *Dictionary of American Scholars.* Lancaster, Pennsyl-
vania: The Science Press, 1951.
Cyclopaedia of American Biography, The. new enl. ed. 6 vols. New York:
Press Associates, Compilers, Inc., 1915.
This work is commonly referred to as "Appleton's Cyclopedia."
Johnson, Allen, and Malone, Dumas (eds.). *Dictionary of American Biogra-
phy.* 22 vols. New York: Charles Scribner's Sons, 1928-1944.
Supplements continue the work.
Who Was Who. 2 vols. Chicago: The Marcus Company, 1942-1950.
Who's Who in America. Chicago: Marcus Who's Who, Inc., 1899—. Published
biennially from 1899 to 1939. Monthly supplements begin in 1939.

7. Guides to Published Government Documents

A. RECORDS OF THE CONGRESS IN CHRONOLOGICAL ORDER

Ford, W. C., and Hunt, Gaillard (eds.). *Journals of the Continental Congresses,
1774-1789.* 34 vols. Washington: Government Printing Office, 1904-1907.
Debates and Proceedings in the Congress of the United States, 1789-1824.
42 vols. Washington: Government Printing Office, 1834-1856.
Compiled by Gales and Seaton, this portion of the records of Congress is
usually referred to as the *Annals of Congress.*
*Register of Debates in Congress, Containing the Debates and Proceedings,
1825-1837.* 29 vols. Washington: Gales and Seaton, editors and publishers, 1825-1837.
Congressional Globe, Containing the Debates and Proceedings, 1833-1873.
109 vols. Washington: F. P. Blair, *et al.*, editors and publishers, 1834-
1873.
Congressional Record, Containing the Debates and Proceedings, 1873—.
Washington: Government Printing Office, 1873—.

B. MATERIALS ON FOREIGN AFFAIRS ARRANGED
CHRONOLOGICALLY

Wharton, Francis. *The Revolutionary Diplomatic Correspondence of the
United States.* 6 vols. Washington: Blair and Rives, 1889.
American State Papers, Foreign Relations, Class I, 1789-1828. Washington:
Lowrie, Gales, and Seaton, editors and publishers.
Hasse, Adelaide R. *Index to United States Documents Relating to Foreign
Affairs, 1828-1861.* 3 vols. Washington: The Carnegie Institution, 1914-
1921.
United States, Department of State. *General Index to the Published Volumes
of the Diplomatic Correspondence of the United States, 1861-1899.*
Washington: Government Printing Office, 1902.
United States, Department of State. *Papers Relating to the Foreign Relations*

of the United States, 1861–. Washington: Government Printing Office.
The series has now reached the 1930's.

United States, Department of State. *Papers Relating to the Foreign Relations of the United States: General Index, 1900-1918.* Washington: Government Printing Office, 1946.
No further indices have been prepared.

Miller, Hunter (ed.). *Treaties and Other International Acts of the United States of America.* Washington: Government Printing Office, 1948.
Continues the *Foreign Relations,* but on a more selected basis.

C. MISCELLANEOUS GOVERNMENT REFERENCES

Boyd, Anne M. *United States Government Publications.* New York: The H. W. Wilson Company, 1949.

Farrand, Max (ed.). *The Records of the First Federal Convention of 1787.* 4 vols. New Haven: Yale University Press, 1911.

Hirshberg, H. S., and Melinat, C. H. *Subject Guide to United States Government Publications.* Chicago: American Library Association, 1947.

Statutes at Large of the United States, 1789-1873. 17 vols. Boston: Little, Brown, 1845-1873.

Statutes at Large of the United States, 1873–. Washington: Government Printing Office, 1875–.

8. Works on Historiography

Anderson, E. N., and Cate, J. L. (eds.). *Medieval and Historiographical Essays in Honor of James Westfall Thompson.* Chicago: The University of Chicago Press, 1938.

Ausubel, Herman, *et al.* (eds.). *Some Modern Historians of Britain.* New York: The Dryden Press, 1951

Barnes, Harry E. *A History of Historical Writing.* rev. ed. New York: Dover Publications, 1961.
First published at Norman: University of Oklahoma Press, 1937.

Bassett, John S. *The Middle Group of American Historians.* New York: The Macmillan Company, 1917.

Bellot, Hugh H. *American History and American Historians.* London: The Athlone Press, 1952.

Engel-Janase, Friedrich. *The Growth of German Historicism.* Baltimore: Johns Hopkins Press, 1954.

Ferguson, W. K. *The Renaissance in Historical Thought.* New York: Houghton Mifflin Company, 1948.

Fitzsimons, Matthew; Pundt, Alfred; and Nowell, Charles (eds.). *The Development of Historiography.* Harrisburg, Pennsylvania: The Stackpole Company, 1954.

Floud, Roderick. *An Introduction to Quantitative Methods for Historians.* Princeton: Princeton University Press, 1973.

Gooch, George P. *History and Historians in the 19th Century.* 2nd ed. London: Longmans, Green, 1913.
Reprinted New York: Peter Smith, 1949.
Covers mainly European historiography but is good on American also.

Halperin, S. William. *Some Twentieth-Century Historians.* Chicago: University of Chicago Press, 1961.

Higham, John; Gilbert, Felix; and Krieger, Leonard. *History.* Englewood Cliffs, New Jersey: Prentice-Hall, Inc., 1965.

Compares European and American historiography—surveys modern trends.

Historical Scholarship in America: Needs and Opportunities. New York: American Historical Association, 1932.

Hutchinson, William T. (ed.). *The Marcus W. Jernegan Essays in American Historiography.* Chicago: The University of Chicago Press, 1937.

Jameson, J. Franklin. *The History of Historical Writings in America.* Boston: Houghton Mifflin Company, 1891.

A classic work but now considerably out of date.

Kraus, Michael. *The Writing of American History.* Norman: University of Oklahoma Press, 1953.

The beginning student is strongly encouraged to prepare for his historical readings by studying this work.

Levin, David. *History as Romantic Art: Bancroft, Prescott, Motely, and Parkman.* Stanford: Stanford University Press, 1959.

Neff, E. *The Poetry of History.* New York: Columbia University Press, 1947.

Powicke, F. M. *Modern Historians and the Study of History.* London: The Odhams Press, 1955.

Robinson, James H. *The New History.* New York: The Macmillan Company, 1916.

Sanders, Jennings B. *Historical Interpretations and American Historianship.* Yellow Springs, Ohio: Antioch Press, 1966.

Schmitt, Bernadotte (ed.). *Some Historians of Modern Europe.* Chicago: The University of Chicago Press, 1942.

Sheehan, Donald H., and Syrett, Harold C. (eds.). *Essays in American Historiography: Papers Presented in Honor of Allan Nevins.* New York: Columbia University Press, 1960.

Shorter, Edward. *The Historian and the Computer: A Practical Guide.* Englewood Cliffs, New Jersey: Prentice-Hall, 1971.

Shotwell, James T. *The History of History.* Vol. I. New York: Columbia University Press, 1939.

This ambitious work is intended to survey the entire course of historical writings throughout the history of civilization. Only the first volume, pertaining to ancient history, has appeared.

Thompson, James W., and Holm, Bernard J. *A History of Historical Writing.* 2 vols. New York: The Macmillan Company, 1942.

Wish, Harvey. *The American Historian: A Social-Intellectual History of the Writing of the American Past.* New York: Oxford University Press, 1960.

Wolman, Benjamin B. (ed.). *The Psychoanalytic Interpretation of History.* New York: Basic Books, 1971.

9. Related Articles in Professional Journals

Beale, Howard K. "What Historians Have Said About the Causes of the Civil War," *Theory and Practice in Historical Study: A Report of the Committee on Historiography.* New York: Social Science Research Council, 1946.

Binkley, William C. "Two World Wars and American Historical Scholarship," *Mississippi Valley Historical Review.* XXXIII (June 1946).

Boyd, J. P. "State and Local Historical Societies in the United States," *American Historical Review.* XL (1934), pp. 10–37.

Ellis, Elmer. "The Profession of Historian," *Mississippi Valley Historical Review.* XXXVIII (1951), pp. 3–20.

Hempel, Carl G. "The Function of General Laws in History," *Journal of Philosophy.* XXXIX (1942), pp. 35–48.

"History and Historiography," *Encyclopedia of the Social Sciences.* 15 vols. New York: Encyclopedia of the Social Sciences, 1930-1935, VII.

Iggers, Georg G. "The Idea of Progress in Recent Philosophies of History," *Journal of Modern History.* XXX (1958), pp. 215-226.

Jameson, J. Franklin. "The Future Uses of History," *American Historical Review.* LXV (1950), pp. 61-72.

Link, Arthur S. "A Decade of Biographical Contributions to Recent American History," *Mississippi Valley Historical Review.* XXXIV (1947), pp. 637-642.

McMurtrie, Donald. "Locating the Printed Source Materials for United States History, with a Bibliography of Lists of Regional Imprints," *Mississippi Valley Historical Review.* XXXI (1944), pp. 369-378.

Nowell, Charles E. "Has the Past a Place in History?" *Journal of Modern History.* XXIV (1952), pp. 331-340.

Ross, E. D. "A Generation of Prairie Historiography," *Mississippi Valley Historical Review.* XXXIII (1946), pp. 391-410.

Schindler, Margaret C. "Fictitious Biography," *American Historical Review.* XLII (1937), pp. 680-690.

Sears, Lawrence. "The Meaning of History," *Journal of Philosophy.* XXXIX (1942), pp. 393-401.

Simkhovitch, Vladimir. "Approaches to History," *Political Science Quarterly.* XLIV (1929), pp. 481-498.

————. "Approaches to History," *Political Science Quarterly.* XLV (1930), pp. 481-527.

Smith, Goldwin. "The Treatment of History," *American Historical Review.* X (1905), pp. 511-520.

Smith, Theodore C. "The Writing of American History in America from 1884 to 1934," *American Historical Review.* XL (1935), pp. 439-449.

Swierenga, Robert P. *"Computers and American History: The Impact of the 'New' Generation," The Journal of American History.* LX (March, 1974).

10. Selected List of Professional Journals

What follows is a typical listing of the various types of professional historical journals currently being published. These journals are particularly important for two reasons: one, they contain many worthwhile professional book reviews, and two, they contain many monographic articles possessing a degree of detail not found in the ordinary textbook.

Since this is only a representative list, the reader is directed to the following sources for detailed and thorough listings of all professional historical publications.

Boehm, Eric, and Lalit, Adolphus. *Historical Periodicals: An Annotated World List of Historical and Related Serial Publications.* Santa Barbara, California: The Clio Press, 1961.

Caron, Pierre, and Jaryc, Marc. *World List of Historical Periodicals.* New York: The H. W. Wilson Company, 1939.

American Archivist.
American Historical Review.
American Jewish Historical Quarterly.
American Political Science Review.
American Scholar.
Annals of the Association of American Geographers.

Business History Review.
Canadian Historical Review.
Catholic Historical Review.
Economic History Review.
English History Review.
Far Eastern Quarterly.
Hispanic American Historical Review.
Historical Bulletin.
Historical Outlook.
History of Education Quarterly.
Journal of American History—formerly the *Mississippi Valley Historical Review.*
Journal of Church and State.
Journal of Modern History.
Journal of Negro History.
Journal of Southern History.
Journal of the History of Ideas.
Library of Congress Quarterly Journal.
Middle East Journal.
New England Quarterly.
New York Times Book Review.
Pacific Historical Review.
Political Science Quarterly.
Proceedings of the American Philosophical Society.
Slavic Review.
Southwestern Social Science Quarterly.

Chronological Tables

Appendix B

This unit contains three major sections. The first gives a scaled representation of the duration of life on this planet in comparison with the lifetime of the earth itself. The second section is an outline chronology of American history, with one column devoted to corresponding key world-developments. And the third section is a chronology of European history.

Chronological tables are as important to the historian as maps are to the geographer or temperature charts are to the physician. They enable the historian to visualize the vast panorama of human history at one sweep. They provide an excellent means of determining time sequence, trends and developments, and the total perspective of human existence.

Time Scale for the History of the Earth

Scale: Each segment equals 100 million years

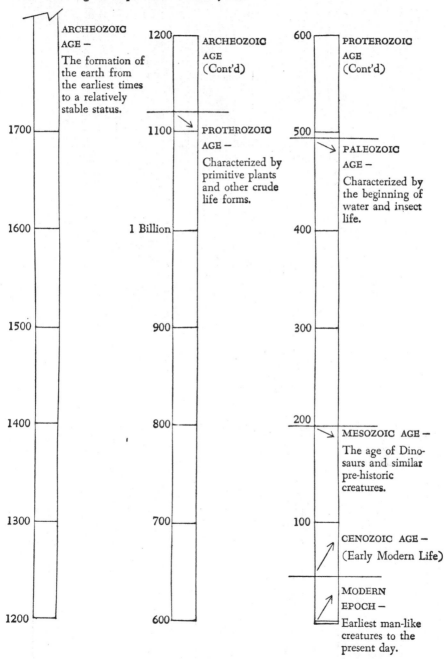

ARCHEOZOIC AGE —
The formation of the earth from the earliest times to a relatively stable status.

1700

1600

1500

1400

1300

1200

1200

ARCHEOZOIC AGE (Cont'd)

1100

PROTEROZOIC AGE —
Characterized by primitive plants and other crude life forms.

1 Billion

900

800

700

600

600

PROTEROZOIC AGE (Cont'd)

500

PALEOZOIC AGE —
Characterized by the beginning of water and insect life.

400

300

200

MESOZOIC AGE —
The age of Dinosaurs and similar pre-historic creatures.

100

CENOZOIC AGE —
(Early Modern Life)

MODERN EPOCH —
Earliest man-like creatures to the present day.

The period dealing with written history cannot be indicated without enlarging this scale hundreds of times.

An Outline Chronology of American History

Date	Event	Non-American
1584–1590	First English attempts at American settlement; Raleigh at Roanoke.	
1588		Defeat of the Spanish Armada.
1607	Jamestown founded—first permanent English New World settlement.	
1608	Quebec founded—first permanent French New World settlement.	
1609	Henry Hudson explores river bearing his name.	
1610	Hudson discovers Hudson's Bay; England claims region.	
1614	Dutch settle trading posts in region of New York.	
1618–1848		Thirty Years War in Europe.
1619	Meeting of first representative assembly in America—Virginia House of Burgesses; slavery introduced.	
1620	Pilgrims land at Plymouth Rock; Mayflower Compact.	
1623	New Hampshire settled. Swedes establish trading posts on the Delaware.	
1626	Dutch establish New Amsterdam (New York).	
1630	Boston settled; Massachusetts Bay Colony founded.	
1634	Maryland founded by Lord Baltimore.	
1635	Connecticut settled.	
1636	Roger Williams expelled from Massachusetts—founds Rhode Island; Harvard College founded.	
1637	Pequot Indian War.	
1638	Swedes establish a colony on the Delaware River.	
1639	The Fundamental Orders of Connecticut.	
1642–1649		England racked by civil war.
1643	Formation of the New England Confederation.	
1643–1715		Louis XIV is King of France.
1649	Maryland Toleration Act	
1655	Dutch seize the Swedish colony on the Delaware.	
1662	Connecticut settlers obtain a charter.	
1663	Rhode Island and Carolina charters granted.	

Date	Event	Non-American
1664	England captures New Amsterdam—renames it New York; New Jersey founded.	
1673	Marquette and Joliet explore the Mississippi River.	
1675	King Philip's Indian War.	
1676	Bacon's Rebellion in Virginia.	
1680	Charleston, South Carolina, settled.	
1681	Pennsylvania founded.	
1682	La Salle journeys the length of the Mississippi River.	
1684–1688	The Dominion of New England.	
1685		Edict of Nantes.
1688		Glorious Revolution in England.
1689	King William's War.	War of the League of Augsburg.
1692	Salem witch trials.	
1693	William and Mary College founded.	
1697	Peace of Ryswick.	Peace of Ryswick.
1701–1713	Queen Anne's War.	War of the Spanish Succession.
1703	Colony of Delaware established.	
1713	Treaty of Utrecht.	Treaty of Utrecht.
1729–1731	North and South Carolina established as separate colonies.	
1733	Colony of Georgia founded.	
1744	Beginning of King George's War.	War of the Austrian Succession.
1748	Treaty of Aix-la-Chapelle.	Treaty of Aix-la-Chapelle.
1754–1763	French and Indian War.	
1756–1763		Seven Years War.
1759	Battle of Quebec.	
1763	Peace of Paris, ending French and Indian War; England begins enforcement of Navigation Acts.	Peace of Paris ends Seven Years War.
1764	Passage of the Stamp Act; arbitrary beginning of the Industrial Revolution.	
1765	Stamp Act Congress.	
1767	Passage of the Townshend Duties.	
1770	Boston Massacre.	
1772–1795		Poland is partitioned.
1773	Boston Tea Party.	
1774	The Intolerable Acts; First Continental Congress.	
1775	Second Continental Congress; Battles of Lexington and Concord.	
1776	Declaration of Independence; Thomas Paine writes *Common Sense*.	Watt invents steam engine.

Date	Event	Non-American
1777	Adoption of the Articles of Confederation; Battle of Saratoga.	
1778	Treaty of Alliance with France.	France goes to war with England.
1779		Spain goes to war with England.
1780		Armed Neutrality of North; England declares war on Holland.
1781	Battle of Yorktown—defeat of Cornwallis.	
1783	End of Revolutionary War; American independence recognized.	
1786	Shay's Rebellion, *Trevett v. Weeden;* Annapolis Convention.	
1787	Constitutional Convention; passage of Northwest Ordinance.	
1789	George Washington becomes first president; first Ten Amendments; first Congress.	Beginning of the French Revolution.
1790	National debt is funded.	
1791	Establishment of First National Bank. Vermont admitted to the Union.	
1793	Eli Whitney invents cotton gin.	Reign of Terror is inaugurated.
1794	Citizen Genet Affair; Whiskey Rebellion; Pinckney's Treaty; Jay's Treaty.	
1797	John Adams becomes second president; XYZ Affair; Alien and Sedition Acts.	
1798	Kentucky-Virginia Resolutions; ratification of Eleventh Amendment.	
1799		Napoleon captures control in France.
1801	John Marshall appointed Chief Justice; Midnight appointment of justices; Jefferson becomes president.	
1801–1805	Tripolitan War.	
1803	Louisiana Purchase; *Marbury v. Madison.*	
1804	Twelfth Amendment ratified.	
1805		Battles of Trafalgar & Austerlitz.
1806		Inauguration of Continental System and Orders in Council.
1807	Fulton develops his steamboat; Chesapeake Affair.	
1809	James Madison becomes president.	
1812		Napoleon invades Russia.

Date	Event	Non-American
1812–1814	War of 1812 with England.	
1814	Treaty of Ghent ends War of 1812; Hartford Convention; Battle of New Orleans.	
1815		Battle of Waterloo; Formation of Holy Alliance.
1816	Establishment of the Second National Bank; first protective tariff passed.	
1817	James Monroe elected president; Seminole Indian War.	
1818	Great Britain and the United States agree on joint occupation of Oregon.	
1819	Adams-Onís Treaty acquires Florida from Spain.	Carlsbad Decrees in Germany.
1821	Completion of the Missouri Compromise.	
1823	Monroe Doctrine enacted to support independence in the Western hemisphere.	
1825	John Q. Adams elected president; Jackson begins the Democratic Party; Erie Canal completed.	
1828	Calhoun's "Exposition of 1828" and the "Tariff of Abominations."	
1828–1829		Russo-Turkish War.
1829	Andrew Jackson elected president—inaugurates the "spoils system."	
1830	Webster-Hayne Debates.	July Revolution in France; railroads in England.
1831	Cyrus McCormick invents the reaper.	
1832	South Carolina threatens secession—nullifies Tariffs of 1828 and 1832.	Reform Bill in England.
1833	Lower tariff heals rift with South Carolina; Jackson declares war on the Second National Bank.	
1835	Texas secedes from Mexico—becomes independent republic.	
1836	Tremendous western inflation and speculation; Specie Circular.	
1837	Martin Van Buren elected president; Panic of 1837.	Queen Victoria begins 64-year reign.
1840	Sub-treasury banking system set up.	
1841	William H. Harrison elected president; dies in office; John Tyler becomes first vice-president to succeed to the presidency under such circumstances.	
1842	Webster-Ashburton Treaty; Preemption Bill.	
1844	Practicality of the telegraph demonstrated.	

Date	Event	Non-American
1845	James Polk elected president; era of Manifest Destiny begins; Texas enters the Union.	
1846	Northern boundary established at 49th parallel by treaty with England; Wilmot Proviso touches off slavery issue.	
1846-1848	The Mexican War.	
1848	Treaty of Guadalupe Hidalgo ends war; Mormans establish in Utah; Free Soil Party if formed.	Revolutions in Austria-Hungary and the Italies— France establishes Second Republic.
1849	Zachary Taylor elected president; gold rush in California.	
1850	Millard Fillmore becomes president upon death of Taylor; Compromise of 1850; Clayton-Bulwer Treaty with England.	
1852	Publication of *Uncle Tom's Cabin;* Franklin Pierce elected president.	
1853	Gadsden Purchase from Mexico.	
1854	Kansas-Nebraska Act; Perry opens Japan; Ostend Manifesto.	
1854-1856		Crimean War.
1856	Summer-Brooks Episode; First Republican convention; "bleeding" Kansas.	
1857	James Buchanan elected President; Dred Scott decision; Panic of 1857.	
1858	Lincoln-Douglas Debates.	First transatlantic cable laid.
1859	John Brown's Raid on Harpers Ferry.	Publication of Darwin's *Origin of Species.*
1860	South Carolina secedes upon Lincoln's election.	
1860-1861		Garibaldi consolidates the Italies.
1861	Lincoln takes office—ten more states secede; Fort Sumter fired upon.	Alexander II frees the Russian serfs.
1861-1865	The American Civil War.	
1862	Battle of Merrimack and Monitor.	
1863	Emancipation Proclamation; Battles of Vicksburg and Gettysburg.	
1863-1867		Maximilian is Emperor of Mexico.
1864	Sherman's March to the Sea.	
1865	Lee surrenders at Appomattox; Lincoln assassinated; Andrew Johnson becomes president; Thirteenth Amendment ratified.	
1866	Civil Rights Act passed; Freedmen's Bureau reestablished.	Austro-Prussian War.

Date	Event	Non-American
1867	Reconstruction Act; Tenure of Office Act; Purchase of Alaska from Russia.	
1868	President Johnson impeached; Fourteenth Amendment ratified.	
1869	Ulysses S. Grant becomes President.	Suez Canal opened.
1870	Fifteenth Amendment ratified.	
1870-1871		Franco-Prussian War; Italy and Germany become united nations.
1871	Treaty of Washington with England.	
1872-1874	Major scandals of Grant regime—Whiskey Ring, Credit Mobilier, etc.	
1873	Financial panic; *Munn v. Illinois.*	
1876	Hayes elected to the presidency in disputed election; Custer's Last Stand; Bell invents telephone.	
1878	Bland-Allison Act.	
1879	Thomas Edison invents electric light.	
1881	Garfield becomes president—assassinated; Chester Arthur assumes presidency; formation of the American Federation of Labor.	
1882		Formation of the Triple Alliance.
1883	Pendleton Civil Service Act passed.	
1885	Grover Cleveland first Democratic president since before the Civil War.	
1886	Haymarket Square Riot.	
1887	Interstate Commerce Act passed.	
1889	Benjamin Harrison becomes president.	
1890	Sherman Anti-trust Act; Sherman Silver Purchase Act; formation of Populist Party; Cleveland becomes president again; Panic of 1893.	
1894	Massive Pullman railroad strike broken by federal troops.	
1894-1895		Sino-Japanese War.
1897	William McKinley becomes president.	Marconi invents wireless telegraph.
1898	Spanish-American War—aquisition of the Philippines, Guam, and Puerto Rico; annexation of Hawaiian Islands.	
1899	Establishment of the Open Door policy.	Hague Conference.
1899-1902		Boer War.
1900	Boxer Rebellion.	Boxer Rebellion.
1901	McKinley assassinated—Theodore Roosevelt becomes President; Hay-Pauncefote Treaty with England.	

Date	*Event*	*Non-American*
1902	Hay—Bunau-Varilla Treaty permits building of Panama Canal.	
1903	Alaskan Boundary dispute with England settled; Wright brothers fly airplane.	
1904–1905		Russo-Japanese War.
1906	Pure Food and Drug Act; Hepburn Act.	
1907		2nd Hague Conference; formation of Triple Entente.
1909	William Howard Taft becomes president.	
1911		Mexican Revolution; Turco-Italian War.
1912	Roosevelt bolts party—forms Bull Moose Party.	
1913	Sixteenth and Seventeenth Amendments ratified; Wilson inaugurated president; Underwood-Simmons Act passed; Federal Reserve System established.	
1914	Clayton Anti-trust Act passed.	
1914–1918		World War I.
1916	Pershing Expedition into Mexico.	
1917	Purchase of Danish West Indies from Denmark; U.S. enters World War I.	
1918	Armistice ending World War I signed.	
1919	Eighteenth Amendment ratified; Versailles Treaty not ratified.	Europe signs Treaty of Versailles.
1920	Nineteenth Amendment ratified.	League of Nations established.
1921	Warren Harding becomes president; Budget and Accounting Act passed.	
1921–1922	Washington Disarmament Conference.	Anglo-Japanese Alliance terminated.
1923	Harding dies—Coolidge assumes the presidency; Gondra Treaty signed; Harding scandals begin to break.	
1924	Johnson Immigration Act establishes quota system.	Dawes Plan for reparations.
1925	Calvin Coolidge attains presidency in his own right.	
1926		British Commonwealth firmly established.
1927	Charles Lindbergh flies Atlantic; Geneva Disarmament Conference fails.	
1928	Kellogg-Briand Peace Pact negotiated.	Young Plan for reparations.
1929	Herbert Hoover inaugurated president; stock market crashes.	Tacna-Arica boundary dispute settled.

Date	Event	Non-American
1930	Hawley-Smoot Tariff passed.	London Naval Conference.
1931–1932		Japan invades Manchuria.
1932	Reconstruction Finance Corporation established to ease depression.	
1933	Franklin Roosevelt becomes president; New Deal inaugurated; Twentieth and Twenty-first Amendments ratified.	Hitler gains control of Germany.
1934	Securities Exchange Commission established; Reciprocal Trade Agreement Act passed.	
1935	Social Security Act and National Labor Relations Act passed.	Italy invades Ethiopia.
1936	Roosevelt overwhelmingly reelected.	Civil war in Spain.
1937	Roosevelt's battle with the Supreme Court.	
1938	Fair Labor Standards Act passed.	Munich pledge.
1939		Germany invades Poland; World War II begins.
1940	Roosevelt elected to a third term; Burke-Wadsworth Act establishes peacetime draft system.	Germany invades France.
1941	Lend-Lease begins; Atlantic Charter signed; Pearl Harbor attacked; U.S. enters World War II.	
1942	Naval battles of Coral Sea and Midway Island.	
1943	Teheran Conference.	Battle of Stalingrad.
1944	Roosevelt elected for fourth term; Normandy invasion; Servicemen's Readjustment Act (G.I. Bill) passed.	
1945	Yalta Conference; atomic bomb exploded; Truman assumes presidency upon the death of Roosevelt; United Nations established; World War II ends.	
1945–1946		Nuremburg War Trials.
1947	Truman Plan; Marshall Plan; Taft-Hartley Act passed.	Formation of Warsaw Alliance.
1949	Truman inaugurated president; North Atlantic Treaty Organization formed:	Communists take over China; Russia explodes atomic bomb.
1950	McCarran Internal Security Act passed; beginnings of McCarthyism.	
1951	Twenty-second Amendment ratified; Korean War begins.	

Date	Event	Non-American
1953	Dwight Eisenhower inaugurated president; Korean War ends.	
1954	Southeast Asian Treaty Organization formed; *Brown v. Board of Education* calls for desegregation.	European Defense Community established.
1955	Salk polio vaccine introduced.	
1956		Suez Canal crisis.
1957	Troops used in Little Rock desegregation.	Russia orbits first Sputnik.
1958	First American satellites orbited.	
1959		Castro takes over Cuba.
1961	John Kennedy inaugurated president; Twenty-third Amendment ratified; an American in suborbit; Peace Corps established; Bay of Pigs incident.	First cosmonaut in space.
1962	Cuban missile crisis.	China invades India.
1963	Kennedy assassinated—Johnson assumes presidency.	
1964	Enactment of War on Poverty program; Civil Rights Act passed; Twenty-fourth Amendment ratified; Gulf of Tonkin Resolution.	
1965	Lyndon Johnson inaugurated president in his own right.	
1966		France pulls out of NATO.
1967	Major riots in American cities.	
1968	Nixon elected president; Martin Luther King and Robert Kennedy assassinated.	Bombing halt over North Vietnam.
1969	First and second moon walks.	
1970	Initiation of Equal Rights Amendment.	Biafran war ends.
1971		Communist China admitted to United Nations.
1972	Nixon reelected president.	Nixon visits Communist China.
1973	Skylab space mission; end to U.S. military involvement in Vietnam.	Arab-Israeli war.
1974	Spiro Agnew resignation; Nixon impeachment inquiry: Nixon resigns—Gerald Ford assumes presidency.	

An Outline Chronology
of Major European Events

Date	Major Events and Developments
B.C.	
2800–1200	Minoan Age in Crete.
2000	The Achaeans colonize Greece.
1600–1500	The Golden Age of Crete.
1500	The Dorian invasion of Greece.
1500–1200	The Mycenaen Age.
1000–900	Etruscans colonize Italy; the Greeks colonize the Aegean Islands; David is king of Jerusalem.
ca. 850	Homer composes the *Iliad* and the *Odyssey*.
845	Carthage founded.
800–600	Age of the Nobles in Greece.
ca. 776	First Olympic Games held.
753	Traditional date for the founding of Rome.
734	Traditional date for the founding of Syracuse.
700–600	The Greeks colonize southern Italy.
650–500	Age of the Tyrants in Greece.
621	Draco writes his Code of Laws.
594	Solon reforms the Athenian constitution.
509	Founding of the Roman republic.
493–479	The Persian Wars: Battle of Marathon (490), Thermopylae (480), and Salamis (480).
444–429	The Golden Age of Pericles—period of Athenian supremacy.
431–404	Peloponnesian Wars: Battle of Aegospotami (405).
404–371	Sparta reigns supreme among the Greek city-states.
390	The Gauls overrun the Romans.
371–362	Thebes is supreme among the Greek city-states.
338	Battle of Chaeronea won by Philip of Macedonia.
338–275	The period of Macedonian supremacy in Greece.
343–341	First Samnite War (Roman).
336–323	Age of Alexander the Great—Hellenistic Period.
326–304	Second Samnite War solidifies Roman power in southern Italy.
290	Third Samnite War ends with the Romans supreme in Italy.
264–241	First Punic War (Rome v. Carthage)—Romans gain Sicily.
218–202	Second Punic War; Hannibal crosses the Alps; Carthage becomes subservient to Rome.
215–206	First Macedonian War.
200–197	Second Macedonian War—Greeks freed from Macedonian rule.
171–168	Third Macedonian War.
149–146	Third Punic War—Carthage destroyed; Macedonia becomes subservient to Rome; Greeks pass under Roman rule. The Greek period ends.
58–51	Julius Caesar conquers Gaul.
44	Caesar is assassinated.
31 B.C.–14 A.D.	Battle of Actium; Octavian rules as Caesar Augustus; the Roman Empire begins; Christ is born.
96–180	Period of the "good" emperors.

Date	*Major Events and Developments*
180-284	Period of general decline; emperors ruled by the army.
284-305	Diocletian is emperor—reorganizes the empire.
311	Christianity is recognized by Galerius; persecutions of Christians cease.
313	The Edict of Milan is promulgated.
323-337	Emperor Constantine reorganizes the empire; moves the capital from Rome to Constantinople (Byzantium).
325	Council of Christian churches at Nicaea.
375	Beginning of the period of barbarian invasions.
378	Battle of Adrianople—the Visigoths defeat the Romans.
379-395	Era of Theodosius the Great, the last Roman emperor to rule a united kingdom. Roman empire divides into east and west in 395, Eastern empire lasts until 1453.
410	Goths led by Alaric sack Rome.
451	Attila the Hun defeated at Châlons.
455	Vandals sack Rome after taking over North Africa.
476	Germanic leader Odovacar deposes the last Roman emperor in the west. Roman period ceases to exist in the west.
481-511	Clovis rules the Merovingian Franks—unites Europe.
493-555	Ostrogoths are supreme in Italy.
511-751	General period of decline for the Merovingians and ascendancy of the Mayors of the Palace.
527-565	Justinian rules eastern Roman empire; issues Justinian Code; conquers the Vandals and the Ostrogoths.
596	Augustine established Christianity among the Jutes, Saxons, and Angles of England.
622	The Mohammedan religion is founded.
687	Battle of Testry—fragmenting Frankish kingdom is reunited.
711	Mohammedans conquer Spain after first overrunning Africa.
732	Charles Martel defeats the Mohammedans at the Battle of Tours—checks the Moorish advance.
751	Pepin creates the Carolingian kingdom.
768-814	Charlemagne rules the Franks and a united Europe; crowned emperor in 800; initiates Carolingian Renaissance.
843	Treaty of Verdun—Europe splits into the crude beginnings of France and Germany.
862	Russia is founded by the Viking, Rurik.
866	The Danes invade England.
871-900	Alfred the Great defeats the Danes and establishes the English kingdom.
936-973	Otto the Great rules Germany; the Holy Roman Empire established (962).
987	Hugh Capet inaugurates the Capetian dynasty in France.
ca. 1000	The Vikings discover North America; feudal system is at its peak in Europe.
1066	Battle of Hastings—the Norman conquest of England.
1075	Investiture struggle between Pope Gregory VII and Henry IV, the Holy Roman Emperor.
1096	Pope Urban II calls for the First Crusade.
1096-1099	The First Crusade—successfully captures Jerusalem.
1122	The Concordat of Worms temporarily solves the investiture struggle.

Date	Major Events and Developments
1147–1149	The Second Crusade—no tangible results.
1152–1190	Frederick Barbarossa is Holy Roman Emperor.
1180–1223	Philip Augustus is king of France; recovers English holdings in Normandy.
1187	Saladin captures Jerusalem.
1189–1192	The Third Crusade—results in negotiated settlement; Christians permitted access to holy places.
1190	Organization of the Teutonic Knights.
1202–1204	The Fourth Crusade—an attempt by the Italians to conquer Constantinople.
1209–1229	Period of dominance of the Albigensian heresy.
1214	Battle of Bouvines; England defeated; Frederick II rules Naples and Sicily as well as the Holy Roman Empire.
1215	King John of England signs the Magna Carta.
1226–1270	St. Louis IX rules France justly.
1228–1229	The Fifth Crusade.
1229	Establishment of the Inquisition.
1272	Edward I, king of England, conquers Wales.
1273–1291	Rudolph of the House of Hapsburg rules Germany following the Interregnum (1254–1273).
1291–1499	Swiss Confederation is developing.
1295	Marco Polo returns from his eastern travels; The English Model Parliament meets.
1297	The fall of Acre brings an end to the Age of the Crusades.
ca. 1300–1500	The period of the Renaissance.
1302	First meeting of the Estates General in France; Battle of Courtrai.
1309–1377	The Avignon Papacy (Babylonian Captivity).
1337–1453	The Hundred Years War between England and France— Battles of Crecy (1346), Poitiers (1356), and Agincourt (1415) on land, and the naval battle of Sluys (1340).
1348	Beginning of the Black Death—spreads from Italy throughout Europe.
1356	Emperor Charles IV issues the Golden Bull.
1378–1417	The Great Western Schism.
1381	Peasant's Revolt in England.
1414–1418	Council of Constance—John Huss burned at the stake for heresy (1415).
1450	Gutenberg invents printing; Jack Cade's Rebellion in England.
1453	Turks capture Constantinople—end Roman empire in the east.
1455–1485	War of the Roses in England.
1485	Battle of Bosworth Field marks the beginning of Tudor rule in England.
1492	Spain completes the Reconquista; Columbus discovers America.
1498	Vasco da Gama reaches India by sailing around Africa.
1509–1547	Reign of Henry VIII in England.
1513–1521	The Medici Pope Leo X encourages the arts.
1517	Luther begins the Protestant Reformation.

Date	Major Events and Developments
1518	Zwingli begins the Reformation in Switzerland.
1519–1522	Magellan circumnavigates the world.
1519–1556	Charles V rules Holy Roman Empire, Spain, Netherlands, and Italy.
1521	Luther condemned by the Diet of Worms.
1525	Peasant's War in Germany.
1536	John Calvin brings the Reformation to Geneva.
1540	Jesuit order founded by Ignatius of Loyola.
1542	Pope Paul III establishes the Italian inquisition.
1545–1563	Council of Trent—the Catholic Counter-Reformation.
1555	The Peace of Augsburg.
1556–1598	Age of Philip II in Spain.
1558–1603	Queen Elizabeth establishes Anglicanism in England; the age of Shakespeare.
1562–1598	Huguenot Wars in France.
1568	Revolt of the Netherlands.
1572	Battle of Lepanto—defeat for the Turks.
1588	Spanish Armada destroyed by England.
1598	Edict of Nantes issued in France.
ca. 1600	Age of Galileo, Harvey, and Kepler.
1607	English under James I found Virginia colony.
1610–1643	Louis XIII rules France with aid of Richelieu.
1611–1632	Gustavus Adolphus is king of Sweden.
1618–1648	Thirty Years War—ends with Peace of Westphalia.
1640–1688	Prussia develops under the rule of the Great Elector.
1642–1649	Civil Wars in England.
1643–1715	Louis XIV rules France—period of French splendor.
1648	Spain recognizes the independence of the Dutch Netherlands.
1653–1658	Cromwell rules England as Lord Protector.
1660	Stuart Restoration in England.
1667–1668	War of the Spanish Netherlands.
1672–1715	Peter the Great begins the westernization of Russia.
1683	John Sobieski, Polish king, halts the Turks at the gates of Vienna.
1685	Revocation of the Edict of Nantes.
1688	Glorious Revolution in England.
1689–1697	War of the League of Augsburg.
1701–1713	War of the Spanish Succession—ends with the Treaty of Utrecht.
1707	Union of England and Scotland.
1713–1740	Frederick William I establishes the Prussian army.
1715–1774	Louis XV rules France.
1740–1748	War of the Austrian Succession.
1740–1780	Maria Theresa rules Austria, Hungary, and Bohemia.
1740–1786	Frederick II expands the Prussian state.
1756–1763	The Seven Years War.
1772–1795	Partitions of Poland (1772, 1793, 1795).
1776	Watt invents steam engine; Adam Smith writes *Wealth of Nations*.
1789	French Revolution begins.

Date	Major Events and Developments
1791	Declaration of Pillnitz; French constitution completed.
1792	Monarchy abolished—France a republic.
1793	Louis XVI beheaded.
1793–1794	Reign of Terror in France.
1795–1799	Rule by the Directory in France.
1796	Napoleon begins Italian compaign—ends with Peace of Campo Formio (1797).
1797	Cisalpine Republic established by Napoleon.
1798	Battle of the Nile—Napoleon defeated.
1799	Napoleon becomes First Consul of France.
1800	Napoleon achieves major victory at Marengo.
1802	Treaty of Amiens.
1804	Napoleon made emperor of France.
1805	Nelson wins Battle of Trafalgar; Napoleon achieves most brilliant victory at Austerlitz.
1806	Confederation of the Rhine formed; Holy Roman Empire dissolved.
1807	Great Britain abolishes slave trade; Peace of Tilsit follows battles of Wagram and Friedland; Alexander I allies with Napoleon.
1812	Napoleon invades Russia; Spanish Penninsular War begins.
1814	Napoleon abdicates—exiled to Elba.
1815	Congress of Vienna; formation of the Holy Alliance; Battle of Waterloo.
1819	German Carlsbad Decrees attempt to stifle liberal ideas.
1821–1829	Greek wars for independence waged successfully.
1828–1829	Russo-Turkish War—ends with Treaty of Adrianople.
1830	July Revolution in France; revolutions in Poland and Italy; Belgium wins independence.
1832	Great Reform Bill passed in England.
1834	Zollverein (German Customs Union) formed.
1837–1901	Queen Victoria rules England.
1840	China opened to foreign trade.
1848	February Revolution in France; revolutions in Sardinia-Piedmont and Austria-Hungary; revolts in the Germanies.
1848–1849	Frankfort Parliament unsuccessfully attempts to unite the Germanies.
1849	Hungarian independence move, led by Kossuth, fails.
1851	Louis Napoleon becomes emperor of France.
1854	Japan opened to foreign trade.
1854–1856	Crimean War.
1858	England assumes jurisdiction over India.
1859	Austro-Sardinian War.
1860–1861	Garibaldi unites most of Italy.
1862	Bismarck assumes power in Germany.
1866	Austro-Prussian War.
1867	Political reform measures in England; Dual Monarchy established.
1869	Suez Canal opened for business.
1870–1871	Franco-Prussian War; Third French Republic proclaimed.
1871	Germany united—German Empire established.

Date	Major Events and Developments
1877–1878	Russo-Turkish War; Congress of Berlin.
1882	Triple Alliance formed; England takes Egypt.
1884	European powers partition Africa.
1891	Dual Alliance established.
1894–1895	Sino-Japanese War; Europe commences dismemberment of China.
1898	Spanish-American War.
1899	First Hague Peace Conference.
1899–1902	England engaged in Boer War.
1900	Boxer Rebellion in China.
1902	Anglo-Japanese Alliance formed; Trans-Siberian Railroad opened.
1904	Entente Cordiale formed; Russo-Japanese War.
1905–1906	First Moroccan Crisis—Algeciras Conference.
1907	2nd Hague Peace Conference.
1908	Period of the Bosnian Crisis.
1908–1909	"Young Turk" movement in Turkey.
1911	Second Moroccan Crisis; Turco-Italian War.
1912–1913	The Balkan Wars.
1914–1918	World War I: assassination of Archduke Ferdinand (1914), Battle of Jutland (1916), Russian Revolution (1917), U.S. enters war (1917), Fourteen Points (1918), Armistice signed (1918).
1919	Treaty of Versailles with Germany—treaties with Austria, Hungary, Bulgaria, and Turkey signed 1919–1920.
1920	League of Nations established.
1921–1922	Washington Disarmament Conference.
1922	Irish Free State established; Mussolini takes over Italy; World Court inaugurated.
1924	Dawes Plan for war reparations.
1925	Locarno Pact signed.
1928	Kellogg-Briand Peace Pact; Young Plan for war reparations.
1928–1932	Russia begins Five Year Plans.
1929	Worldwide depression begins.
1930	France evacuates the Rhineland.
1931	King deposed—Spain becomes a republic.
1931–1932	Japan invades Manchuria.
1933	Third Reich established by Hitler.
1935	Germany remilitarizes.
1936	Germany reoccupies the Rhineland; Italy seizes Ethiopia; Civil War begins in Spain.
1938	Munich Pact signed; Germany annexes Austria.
1939	Fascists win civil war in Spain; Germany seizes Czechoslovakia and invades Poland; Italy annexes Albania; World War II begins in Europe.
1941	Germany invades Russia; Japan attacks Pearl Harbor; United States enters conflict; Atlantic Charter signed.
1942	Naval battles of Coral Sea and Midway Island.
1942–1943	Battle for North Africa.
1943	Battle of Stalingrad; surrender of Italy.
1944	France liberated; Germany invaded.

Date	Major Events and Developments
1945	Germany surrenders; atomic bombs dropped on Japan; Yalta Conference; Japan surrenders; San Francisco Conference establishes United Nations.
1946	Fourth French Republic proclaimed.
1947	Establishment of Pakistan and India as independent countries.
1948	Israeli nation established; enactment of the Marshall Plan; Organization of American States established.
1949	North Atlantic Treaty Organization formed; Council of Europe created; Communists take over China.
1950	South Korea invaded—Korean War begins.
1951	World War II peace treaty with Japan signed.
1953	Death of Stalin.
1954	Southeast Asian Treaty Organization formed; Indochina conflict.
1955	Geneva Conference completed; Warsaw Pact signed; Bagdad Pact negotiated.
1956	Suez Canal Crisis; Hungarian Revolution.
1957	First man-made satellite (Russian) placed in orbit.
1958	Creation of the Fifth French Republic under De Gaulle.
1959	China infringes upon Indian borders as outgrowth of Tibet conflict; European Free Trade Association established.
1960	Congolese Civil War.
1961	First cosmonaut in space; Berlin Crisis.
1962	Cuban missile crisis; Russia breaks test ban.
1963	Atmospheric nuclear test ban negotiated; President Kennedy assassinated.
1964	Gulf of Tonkin Resolution.
1966	France pulls out of North Atlantic Treaty Organization.
1967	Mideast Crisis flares up.
1968	Russia invades Czechoslovakia; European monetary crisis.
1969	Charles De Gaulle resigns.
1970	Biafran war ends.
1971	Communist China admitted to United Nations.
1972	U.S. president visits Communist China.
1973	Arab-Israeli war; Arab oil embargo; energy crisis.

Index

2 3 4 5 6 7 8 9 10 –GBC– 80 79 78 77 76 75